EXODUS

EXODUS   **EXODUS**

A Book for Black Americans
Suggesting a Way Out and Up

EXODUS

B.B. Robinson

©Copyright

Brooks B. Robinson
BlackEconomics.org
P.O. Box 8848
Honolulu, HI 96830-8848
December 2020

ISBN: 9798587412750

Dedication

To the religious organizations (The Church of God by Faith and the Nation of Islam) that nurtured, validated, and taught me in my youth about the *Exodus*.

To my grandchildren, who will live Black America's exodus.

And to those who are doers of the word, not readers only.

Foreword

It is often the role of economists, historians, political scientists, even sociologist to characterize a people. Sometimes, however, even philosophers characterize a people accurately. A case in point is the characterization of Black Americans as "People of the Dust." "A Dust People." That was the phrase adopted by the late religious philosopher, Warith Deen Mohammed, to characterize Black Americans shortly after he took control of the then Nation of Islam following the passing of his father, Elijah Muhammad, in 1975.

Why did Mohammed adopt this phrase? Because Black Americans are carried from point-to-point, place-to-place by the wind powers of the world. Arguably, we are part of the development of those winds when we initiate new fads. The important point is that, as the world lives through new and changing fads, we are moved by those fads. During our 400-plus year sojourn in North America we have been driven to respond to the winds of Slavery, Reconstruction, Black Codes, Jim Crow and Lynchings, Civil Rights, the War on Crime and Black Incarceration, Rap and Gangsta Rap eras, the Dot.com era, the Great Recession, the Covid-19 Pandemic with George Floyd's murder, and who knows what is next on the horizon. We have had little control over our actions. We have been mainly reacting. Like dust, we have been carried along—without much of a definitive shape because our shape keeps changing.

Is it not time that we add water, that is knowledge, to the dust so that we can shape our mud into a real living (clay) being that can decide and move on its own to its predetermined state or position? By adding proper knowledge (water) we exit the dust: Exodus. We become a people with goals and aspirations that are not determined by others, but that are determined by us. In other words, we need to exit the dust so that we can become the real us for us by us.

An individual can be forward leaning and thinking—searching the horizon for potentially favorable avenues to follow to arrive at a favorable state. That individual can add to the thoughts of other individuals, who have performed essentially identical exercises. Ultimately, however, we must evolve a mechanism for synthesizing those futuristic thoughts so that they become achievable goals/aspirations with paths that take us there. To realize this process, we need our own uninterrupted space. So, potentially, one of the first objectives should be to create that space. We already know that it is exceedingly difficult—nearly impossible—to create that space within the borders of what is now the United States of America, which is controlled completely by others.

Therefore, our minds should lead us to the more traditional interpretation of exodus: "To go out." Is it not reasonable that we should design a plan to go out partly or completely to that space that will allow us to create a future that we desire? Yes! Now you have arrived at the reason for this small book. It provides considered rationales for departing and provides some insights concerning ways to go out. But this is only the first step of a broader long-term strategic plan to get us where we want to go.

We hope that you will see and use this book as a solid starting point for changing the course of history for Black Americans and, thereby, human history. Once you grasp the essential nature of the exodus that we propose and concur, then we hope that you will pass these ideas along to other so that a true exodus can be achieved.

Table of Content

Chapter One: Introduction 1

Chapter Two: Once a Slave, Forever a Slave? 5

A Meditation 5

Preliminaries 5

Definition of Terms 7

Introduction 7

Big and Not So Big Questions 11

Doing for Self 13

Remaining a Slave 16

For Those Who Want Freedom 18

Conclusion 20

Chapter Three: All it Takes Is One 23

Meditation 23

Introduction 23

The Power of One 25

Long- Awaited Justice 26

Exodus' Hebrews and Egyptians 27

India's Hindus and Muslims 28

Rwanda's Tutsis and Hutus 30

Bosnia-Herzegovina's Muslims and Christians 32

Sri Lanka's Sinhalese and Tamils 36

Sudan's North and South 40

The Best Option 42

Conclusion 43

Chapter Four: Nation Formation Through Migration 45

Introduction 45

North, Central, and South American Nation Formation 46

Emigration Today 46

Recent Nation Formation and Immigration 48

Immigrants in Nations' Populations Today 48

India's Partition and Black American Nation Formation 50

Conclusion 53

Chapter Five: Future Black Independent Living in the US . 54

Introduction 54

Assumptions 55

Precursor Considerations 57

Choosing Territories 59

Selecting a Territory to Grab 63

The Economy of the Territories 65

Conclusion 74

Appendix A.—List of Fundamental Migration Variables and Their Interpretations. 77

Appendix B.—Sources: Migration Variables Statistics 80

Appendix C.—Summary of Migration Statistics by State . 85

Appendix D.—State-Wise Ranking of Unweighted Migration Variables 87

Chapter Six: Point Zero Nation Formation Revisited 89

Introduction 89

Reparatory Justice 90

    Administrative Aspects of Nation Formation 92

    Shabazzland's/Zion's Socioeconomic Framework 95

    Phased Actualization of Shabazzland/Zion 101

    Conclusion 103

Chapter Seven: Exodus or Else 105

Index 112

List of Tables

Table 1.—Top 10 Emigrant Countries of Origin and the US 47
Table 2.—Top 10 Countries with Stocks of Immigrants by Size
.... 49
Table 3.—High Black Population Percentage States 59
Table 4.—States that Black Americans Could Control with a
Two Million or Less Black American Migration 60
Table 5.—A State-Wise Index of Ranked Migration Variables 64

List of Figures

Figure 1.--Pathway to Shabazzland's/Zion's Development 93

Chapter One: Introduction

How did we get into this predicament?

One can argue unequivocally, and Lindsey "Rob" Robinson has made a nearly airtight case, that we were never slaves.[1] Rather, we were kidnapped and imprisoned without due process and brought to the wilderness of North America. But to simply argue that case is like "crying over spilled milk." What we must do is address the pain that lingers to this day in connection with slavery. That is our starting point. It is how we got ourselves into this predicament. Consequently, our first step on the journey to exodus is to start with the conscious mind and convince it that: (1) We were never slaves; and (2) just because we were called "slaves," that label does not define our future. This line of reasoning might seem elementary in 2021 when there are Black American billionaires. However, when you read the second chapter of this book you will comprehend why it is so critical to start with the question: "Once a slave, forever a Slave?"

Assuming that we are able to answer the foregoing question with a resounding and definitive "NO," then we can go further in an analysis that can get us to exodus. What is the next step in the analysis? It is to observe our environment in its rich historical context and decide that the set of circumstances in which we have found ourselves with White Americans over and over again does not bode well for a tenable and stable equilibrium. That is, even if we were foolishly kind enough to forgive White America for all of its egregious sins, there is a high probability that at some point

---

[1] Lindsey "Rob" Robinson. (2020) "Never a Slave." BlackEconomics.org. September 14. https://www.blackeconomics.org/BEMedia/nas.pdf; retrieved on October 6, 2020.

in the future, a young Black American boy or girl will read the history and say: "I know what White America did to my great, great, great grandfather and grandmother and I stake my life on making White America pay." On the other hand, when Black America rises to supersede White America at some point in the future, then the reverse is likely to occur. A young White boy or girl will say: "I know that my great, great, great grandfather and grandmother owned Black Americans, you are nothing but a slave, and I am going to return you to your former state." So, no matter how you consider the possibilities—one side or the other—it leads to a contentious mental and physical battle based on the history. If you do not believe that Blacks and Whites living together in America is such an untenable and unstable condition, then we provide Chapter Three entitled "All it Takes is One."

Chapter Four is intended to provide assurance that Black America can exodus successfully. In it we discuss: (i) The role of migration in nation formation—particularly in the Americas; (ii) the volume of emigrants in the world today; (iii) the fact that the most-recently formed nations have not relied heavily on immigration; (iv) the role of immigrants in nations' populations today—particularly the US; and (v) the case of India's Partition, which is a clear case of nation formation through migration. The main thrust of Chapter Four is to show that migration can enable a people to separate themselves from their nemeses and seek improved well-being. Of course, when Black America migrates in search of freedom and independence it could mark the largest migration in recent history. The chapter reveals that migrations are a natural phenomenon, and that we can operationalize successful nation formation effort through migration if the process is planned well.

Chapters Five ("Future Black Independent Living in the US") and Six ("Point Zero Nation Formation Revisited") provide two scenarios under which Black Americans can essentially exodus from White America. In the first case (Chapter Five), we describe how Black America can logically migrate to one or more selected states in the country that have minimal White majority population size. Given that these selected states have a White majority population of about one million or less, it seems reasonable that we can migrate in sufficient numbers to these states, swamp the White population, and capture control of these territories—making them all Black states over time for all intents and purposes.

In the second case (Chapter Six), we consider prospects for an agreement between White and Black America in a reparations context. However, unlike the folly of many reparationists today, we recognize that it is highly unlikely that White America can or will extend trillions of dollars to Black America in a one-time or series of payments. On the other hand, if conditions evolve favorably for Black Americans, then it is possible that White America might agree to extend payment to Black Americans in the form of land for the egregious and incalculable historical wrongs done. With such land in hand Black America can embark on a journey of fashioning our own independent living arrangement.

In both cases one and two we go into considerable details discussing how all of this is possible. At the same time, we recognize that this book cannot provide the level of intricate details that would be required to provide a complete roadmap for the two types of exodus. Nor should it. One cannot today predict with explicit and complete specificity all of the circumstances that will exist when our actual exodus commences. This book is designed to open us up to the possibilities of exodus. The precise exodus roadmap will be fashioned by those who embark upon it and work to materialize it.

Chapter Seven, which is entitled "Exodus or Else," summarizes and concludes. It is our final opportunity to convince you that Black America should be exploring every opportunity to exodus each day of our lives. The evidence is transparent to support us that, if Black America does not exodus, then our over 400-year sojourn in America will have been for naught. What a sad tale that would be.

We entered the land, served as unpaid and underpaid labor that built America's "pyramids." We swelled in population to the point of becoming troublesome. Pharoah and his associates have implemented many tricks to destroy us, especially Black American males. The calamities have come: Extreme cold; ice; extreme heat; floods; hurricanes, tornadoes, fires, and viral pestilence. We are nearing the point when the call will be made to rise and join the road to exodus. Let us not waiver or fatigue. Rather, let us be strengthened by the knowledge that we have knowledge and power to realize our long-held aspiration: The making of a peaceful abode in this land ("a promised land") where we can all live in harmony as one because we will be one Black American nation. And if Hebrews deserved to be awarded Israel as a promised land, then the same must be made true for Black Americans. But to get to the promised land—there must be exodus.

You may not want to exodus because you love America. However, there should be no major loss to you to support your fellow Black Americans who want to go out. At a minimum, you should avoid opposing Black Americans who want to do and get something for self. Let whomsoever will come and join the exodus.

Chapter Two: Once a Slave, Forever a Slave?

A Meditation

There is the question: "Should Black Americans be known as slaves?" The answer is "No." Why? Because we were never slaves. We were kidnapped from the African continent and imprisoned without due process. We had committed no crime. The crime was committed against us. Nevertheless, in the current history written mainly by White America (and in many cases adopted by Black Americans), we are known as having been slaves. It is imperative that we push back on that history and the reference that we were "slaves." We can operationalize that push back in many ways, including by writing and socializing our own history. We will be most able to achieve the latter outcome in our own nation after we exodus White America. But to get to that point, we must first undo our "slavery" mindset.

This chapter came during September 2020. It is a psychoanalytical exercise in the form of an essay that begins with a critical question: "Once a slave, forever a slave?" It reminds us that we must first get our mind right before we can embark on the exodus journey.

Preliminaries

"Once a slave, forever a slave?" It is a question that warrants consideration by Black Americans because we have lived under actual, and strong remnants of, slavery for over 400 years. While new slaves or those whose slavery is short-lived possess the impetus to strike out vigorously for a return to freedom, those who endure slavery for an elongated period may be lulled into an acceptance of their condition and lose the urgency to seek freedom. Is it possible to be a slave for so long as to forget what it means to be free? Can one become so conditioned to a life of slavery or the semblance of freedom that, although one may have a sense that one should be free, the burning desire for freedom disappears? Has our stock of cultural capital, which enters our freedom and independence production function, become so devoid of freedom and independence factors that we can no longer actually produce freedom and independence?

Given that Black Americans have failed to achieve true freedom and independence from our White masters for such a long time, these questions must comprise an essential part of our consideration as we make half-hearted efforts to modify the slave system in which we live, as opposed to breaking completely free from it. Do we continue to make these superficial efforts just to confirm that we are "trying to be free?" We certainly do not issue the cry: "Freedom or death!"

Some may argue that the latter cry is foolish. Better to live as a slave than to die free. It is a personal choice. However, considering that Black Americans **on the whole** have not taken time to formulate and implement radical yet reasonable strategies to gain freedom that may not bring us to the point of death, it seems that, maybe, we really do not have a strong interest in being free and independent.

Let us explore these issues to determine whether we really want freedom; whether we can summon the wherewithal to design a strategy that will take us to freedom; or whether we have become comfortable with our plight, as problematic as it may be, because the agonizing pressure of slavery for over 400 years is just too much to overcome. In other words, let us find the answer to the question: Once a slave, forever a slave?

Definition of Terms

"Freedom" and "independence" are used liberally throughout. Therefore, it is appropriate to provide operational definitions of these terms.

Freedom.—Freedom is to possess power to be the ultimate decider/determiner and doer. Being permitted poetic license for individual, creative expression within selected components of life's games and subgames is not freedom. Rather freedom is the power to determine the structure and rules of the components of life's games and subgames—indeed, of the game of life itself as it is known in an established society.

Independence.—Independence is being unchallenged in establishing and evolving a society. A declaration of independence is insufficient. Those who are independent not only declare their independence, but they also sustain their society without unwelcomed interference by outsiders by force of law and/or might.

To the casual observer it is clear that Black America—a nation within a nation—is neither free nor independent. All of our waking and sleeping moments in life reflect our acting, dancing, and singing to White America's tune.

Introduction

The essence of man is his mind—his psychology. A critical psychological component of man's evolution is conditioning. Of course, there are human instincts. But much of our behavior hinges on our conditioning. Consequently, we propose to replace the dichotomy "nature versus nurture" with "instincts versus conditioning." Human development psychologists may contend that there is no distinct difference between "nature versus nurture" and "instinct versus conditioning."

We all know that Black America is in a quandary. There is the important question of what we are going to do about addressing anti-Black racism in America? We cannot escape the persistent anguish, pain, and suffering that accompanies our lives in this wilderness. Some Black Americans (the better-off) may argue that they have no anguish, pain, or suffering. But even they must acknowledge the anguish that is elicited while driving on a lone dark road when Black man/woman meets police or vigilante. Also, there is all of the emotional pain associated with "XXX While Black." So, we will disabuse better-off Blacks that they experience no anguish, pain, or suffering. Not-so-well-off Blacks rush to agree about the anguish, pain, and suffering on all fronts. They are the poster children of poverty, ignorance, and fear. Given these plights, we seek reasonable responses to the quandary using the Socratic Method.

Why are Blacks faced with this dilemma or quandary? There are many answers. Educator historian Dr. Claud Anderson argues that we face this situation because Black America is weak.[2] Philosopher Cornel West argues that Blacks and Whites are all in it together, and that the cause of the anguish, pain, and suffering is autocrats and plutocrats who sit on piles of wealth at the top leaving the middle class and the poor without much hope of transforming the system.[3] West says that those at the top have lost their humanity. Economics Professors William Darity and Darrick Hamilton conclude that economic inequality and anti-Black racism are at the origin of our anguish, pain, and suffering.[4]

---

[2] Claud Anderson. (2001) *PowerNomics: The National Plan to Empower Black America*. PowerNomics Corporation of America, Inc.: Bethesda.
[3] Cornel West. (2004) *Democracy Matters: Winning the Fight Against Imperialism*. Penguin Books: New York.
[4] William Darity, Jr., Darrick Hamilton, *et al.* (2018) *What We Get Wrong About the Racial Wealth Gap*. Samuel DuBois Cook Center on

The next logical question is: Now that we know at least some of the causes of our quandary, what are we going to do about it? All of the aforementioned experts lean on the current social, political, and economic systems to provide a solution. Unfortunately, systems that created past and create current conditions are usually impotent to produce novel avenues out of the quandary. Since the Slavery Era, Black Americans have collaborated with other groups in America to attempt to create change through the existing system. None of the efforts were fully successful. It seems that those operating in the system (American capitalism), who have been conditioned by and through the system, are unable to envision an effective strategy for convincing all in the system to change.

So, if we understand our quandary, know the causes of it, but are unable to change it because of conditioning by and within the system, then we are left with at least one logical alternative: To create change through a new and radical process—namely inventing new wine and new skins. Alas, we are left with another question: How do we make new wine and new skins?

This returns us to the issue of our human psychology. Throughout the course of human history, only geniuses have been able to invent novel ideas (new wine and new skins). We have already concluded that what we need today are geniuses who can: (i) Create new avenues of change that bypass existing conditioning and that are acceptable by, or can be imposed on, all of those in the system; and (ii) who

---

Social Equity and Insight Center for Community Economic Development. https://socialequity.duke.edu/wp-content/uploads/2019/10/what-we-get-wrong.pdf; retrieved on November 29, 2020.

can create a new system that will resolve Black America's quandary.

So, now that we know how new wine and skins can be made, why is it so difficult to produce them? Well, it appears that we are entering a type of inferential loop. It is difficult to imagine a new system—not tweaks of the existing system at the margin—while in an existing system because the existing system has conditioned us to accept it with all of its warts. Even those who are dissatisfied have developed coping mechanism to accept the system as it is. Black America copes, as does White America, by consumerism (shopaholism), drug addiction, over-eating (gluttony), sexual addiction, sports addiction, music fanaticism, videogame addiction, geekism, etc.—all conditioned in us by the system. We may say that we hate the system, but we find ways to "enjoy" life while in the system. Therefore, we are unable to engineer a radical enough act that will break us and others out of the system's grasp.

It is reasonable to expect that Black America should see that the current system is bent on optimizing the material. A simple, but radical reversal would be to optimize an alternative. Even the small and poor nation of Bhutan has agreed that materialism is not an optimal outcome and has agreed to optimize happiness. On the surface, Black America's revealed preference appears to be to optimize altered states that are realized through the aforementioned addictions. At least we flail in our helplessness to express our discontent, but without a truly rational response.

At bottom we are now asking the question for Black America: If you are once a slave, are you always a slave? This is a logical question given that we have not been able to break sufficiently free of the system to generate a new and rational reality for ourselves in the nation proper. Even the wealthy ones among us are all slaves of the larger, wealthier White powers in the system. Those free-wheeling Black entrepreneurs among us (especially those who operate other-than-service enterprises) produce nearly nothing and stand at the mercy of those White enterprises that produce goods that the former are relegated to simply buy and sell. So, all Blacks in America are essentially slaves—even after the Civil War, Reconstruction, Jim Crow, Civil Rights, and BLM Eras. We are positioned to play little-to-no role in determining which outcomes are desired for the society, what is produced by the society, or how that production is employed to produce desired outcomes for the society.

It appears that we have little recourse, at least until a genius arrives who has a sufficiently elevated intellect to convince the powers that be that it is in the latter's best interest to permit the reconditioning of all in the system. This would be a massive undertaking that involves not only the United States but the entire known world. The reference to the "world" is very pertinent because it is transparent that, through globalization, the entire world has wittingly or unwittingly chosen to optimize the material and has evolved a system of masters and slaves. Therefore, it will take no ordinary transformation to undo the current world system, initiate a new course for human life on the planet, and reach a blissful state. It is certainly a tall order for Black America to lead such a transformation. But we should not underestimate our potential.

Big and Not So Big Questions

There are the big questions, such as: Are we alone in the universe? What is man's purpose on Earth? But there are smaller, especially important questions that lead to more questions for which answers are apparent in human history. For example, because we know of only a very few who have had an opportunity to leave Earth's atmosphere—and then only to reach space or go to the Moon—we should ask: Is it possible that many of us will ever depart the planet for other celestial destinations? The practical answer for at least the next few generations is likely to be "no." In other words, no matter the measure of our displeasure, except for *Hari Kari*, we are left with the prospect of living out our unpleasant life on this rock somewhere in the universe.

If we humans cannot actually leave Earth, then we must reside here in peace. The alternative is a world destroyed by nuclear conflict or a dramatic poisoning of the atmosphere, water, or earth, which could bring life as we know it to an absolute or near conclusion. Therefore, if we are to live in peace on planet Earth with the level of knowledge and awareness available today, then there must be compromise.

In an era of compromise, who is going to lead Earth's inhabitants intellectually and materially? The Western World has played this role for recent centuries. But this may change in the not too distant future. In fact, we know from human history that leadership (material and intellectual) has shifted from time to time and from location to location. Hence, it should not be a surprise to anyone that it is about to shift again. This natural shifting through competition and discovery is not problematic unless and until a declining leadership seeks to prevent this natural arising of new leadership. We can only hope that there are no deleterious efforts to halt or hamper the forthcoming shift in world leadership.

In the US, there is also a need for an important shift. The relevant analogy is that of a growing child in a family. The family secures the child's growth until maturity, then releases that child to find its way in the world—standing in the background to offer a supporting hand should needs arise. Black America has been that child for the nation. Our numbers have ballooned from just a score in 1619 to nearly 45 million in 2020. It is time for the Black American child to leave White America's home to identify and build a home and way in the world of our own. Just as efforts should not be directed at halting the global shift in leadership, no efforts should be undertaken to halt Black America's search for, and operationalization of, freedom and independence.

Black America has acquired knowledge and awareness sufficient to build and operate our own nation. We are bursting, at least conceptually, with a desire for independence. A thwarting of this inclination to become independent will likely stifle our ambition to grow and develop properly, making us a considerable weight on White America's shoulder. The latter outcome can only result in an acceleration of America's slowdown and decline.

The key not-so-big question in this case is whether Black America can break the chains that link us in every respect to White America and forge a path to freedom and independence—one that does not lead to our demise, but that takes us to a new land of promise that incorporates features that are beneficial for us and the entire world?

Doing for Self

It could be true that "once a slave, always a slave." On the other hand, many slaves have found ways to fight back and escape. Admittedly, outcomes after escapes have been mixed. But in the grand scheme of things we know that each escape began with a plan. Where is Black America's plan to escape?

From the outset of Black post-15th century presence in North America, slaves have found ways to plan their escape. In

2020, given Black America's knowledge, it should be a small challenge to assemble ingenious minds to formulate a strategy of escape and survival beyond the walls of White America. As we have said so often, we should not expect to do the same thing over and over again yet expect different results. If we want new results, then we must do something different. In this case, a logical alternative is to opt for nation formation. And, if not nation formation, then at least pseudo independent state formation.

To envision new results, however, one must possess a new mind. An important and undergirding question in this chapter is whether Black America can undergo a parthenogenesis that produces a new mind within us. This would be a novel occurrence because we have for over 400 years been on the unfavorable end of a master-slave relationship. Not only has servitude been taught to us, but it has been imposed and reinforced minute by minute, day by day, and year by year for over 400 years. Clearly, the master is benefiting from this relationship, has no intention of undermining his position, and seeks to continually condition us to remain in place. Can a parthenogenesis "miracle" occur?

Chapter Five discusses how seemingly easy it would be for Black America to secure a foothold of independence by occupying (migrating to) sparsely populated states.

We migrated by the millions from south to north during the middle part of the 20th century. Toward the latter part of the 20th century, we began a migration by the millions from north to south to escape a rusting of the northern economy, to renew familial ties, and to benefit from an economically growing south. It is shameless and thoughtless that Black American leadership is so conditioned as to be unable to see the benefits of operationalizing migrations to sparsely populated states (e.g., Montana, Wyoming, North Dakota, or South Dakota) where Blacks could easily gain considerable independence and power.

It is ironic that our leadership can call for a Million Man March and can organize BLM demonstrations all over the country, but we cannot see the benefits of motivating millions of unemployed Blacks (young and old) to migrate to new areas of the country to assume control and build Black dominated states. But of course, to effect all of these outcomes you need a new mind and a plan.

Obviously, one would not expect "front line" organizations, such as the NAACP, National Urban League, NAN, and, the BLM Movement to develop the type of strategic plan that would place Black America on a path to real independence and social, political, and economic power and success in America. Also, it appears to be asking too much to expect Black religious leadership to develop such a plan. But it is unexpected that in their nearly 200-year history HBCUs, which should engender the formation of new minds, have not awarded a degree for a long-term strategic plan (LTSP) for Black America. This appears to be a gross dereliction of duty. Think of the great Howard University. It, too, has no LTSP for Black America—even with its highly touted Political Science, Economics, and Civil Engineering programs. Again, the conditioning within all of these organizations and educational institutions has tilted the outcome toward the status quo.

So, we issue this appeal to awaken within the hearts and minds of those not so deeply conditioned as to not be able to envision a new future. They must birth within themselves the motivation to gain the knowledge required to develop and implement a LTSP that we need direly and that will lead to freedom and independence.

This is an urgent appeal because the evolution of technology is occurring at breakneck speed. Given the individualization of learning through Jane/John Doe's most ubiquitous learning tool (i.e., the Internet) and related efforts to control it by government and monopoly business, it may not be long before it becomes nearly impossible to derive novel/radical thought intended to truly supplant the status quo amidst the labyrinth of artificial intelligence's tracking, echo chambers, confirmation bias, and the like.

Remaining a Slave

If Black America fails to obtain independence, then what will transpire?

No doubt dissatisfaction will continue, which means that cycles of protest and pacification will continue for Black America. But as we know from the 155-year post-Civil War American History these cycles result in marginal progress at best for Black America. Therefore, the reality of a Black upper, middle, and lower class will remain, with the latter suffering egregiously from poverty, ignorance, and fear. This fear could become heightened over time and produce progressively intensified protests. Such reaction will cause the police state to exact more blood and impose more deaths. Rest assured, however, that White, racist America will remain in control.

If Black America begins to serve as a heavy burden on America's economic system, then efforts will be accelerated to dispense with those Blacks who do not serve White America's interests—especially the poor, ignorant, and the "too intelligent." Whether it be through drugs, vaccines, viruses, incarceration or outright murder by the police, there are always ways to dispense with the unwanted even as the world looks on.

America may adopt the just delineated or other approaches to addressing the "Black American Problem" because the former wants to maintain her position as a world leader. It is worth mentioning that China was one of the first to comment that America's decline in elementary and secondary educational performance was due to Black America's poor educational performance. Be assured that America took note of China's comment and understands the toll of dead weight.

For those remaining Black slaves, amalgamation will facilitate their slow disappearance from the landscape. It is already the case that nearly one quarter of newly married Black males marry outside of the race. Also, a check of recent media (print and electronic) will clue you in on a new and increasing thrust to convince marrying age Black American females (over 50 percent of whom never marry) to couple with White males. It should not take too many generations to see the disappearance just referenced.

For those Blacks who result from White and Black mixed unions and who reflect a Black phenotype, their plight will not be much improved from that of their all Black predecessors—they will remain at the bottom of the socioeconomic ladder. However, for those who come away with a Eurocentric phenotype, their plight is likely to be improved significantly. This is more so the case if the latter are extended Eurocentric names. But even this turn of events will find both the predominantly Black and White phenotype offspring trapped in a world of materialism, where they serve mainly as slaves to rich and powerful masters who care little-to-nothing about their existence.

For Those Who Want Freedom

For Black Americans who want freedom and independence, the challenges are great—both the envisioning of a new reality and the effort required to achieve it practically.

Those Blacks who believe that the U.S. Government—at whose feet a reparations bill must be placed—will make available more than ten trillion reparations dollars to Black America are living a fantasy. And, in the strange event that reparations are paid, then you can be assured that the payment will come ensconced in transactions that produce unfavorable outcomes for Black America. It will be another of the dirty tricks that Whites have played on Blacks throughout the course of their association.[5]

If, on the other hand and under special circumstances, White America chooses to permit our exodus and assists us through large land grants, then this may prove to be a satisficing outcome.

Note the operative clause, "special circumstances." One such circumstance would be where the "chickens come home to roost." That is, America has played a central role in the physical destruction (creative though it may be) of many countries all around the world during the last half century: e.g., Vietnam, Iraq, Libya, Afghanistan, etc. It would be just desserts if Black America comes to realize our true worth and the importance of, and right to, our freedom and adopts

---

[5] For an analysis of potential adverse outcomes from cash reparations payments, see Brooks Robinson (2020), "Book Review: From Here to Equality: Reparations for Black Americans in the 21st Century," (May 10th). https://www.blackeconomics.org/BELit/br-fhte.pdf; retrieved on November 10, 2020.

a position of "freedom at all costs," then America might receive a serious, if not deadly, dose of its own medicine. It is not unrealistic that dispossessed and disenchanted Black Americans (young and old) come to adopt the position of those suicide bombers who we have heard and read so much about over the past two decades. If this reality unfolds, then White America will find war in her own living room. If this war cannot be controlled, then the final solution may come in the form of land grants for a separate Black American territory in what is now the United States.

Realize that we are essential workers everywhere and have access to much of the nation's critical infrastructure and operations. Even the threat that Black America is disenchanted enough and has learned how to prosecute war (we comprise continuously about 17 percent of the nation's military) should be sufficient for White America to consider prospective outcomes, acquiesce, and concur on our freedom and independence.

To forget the Christopher Jordan Dorner story might constitute a fatal error. Mr. Dorner sought justice.

Whether understood spontaneously, or derived from high moral or religious teachings, fully comprehending (meditating on) the incalculable injustices that Blacks have endured for over 400 years in America might provide the divine spark that serves as the seed for a new mind for Black American "slaves." If this seed germinates in the rich soil of the Black American nation, then a new mind can come forth. The new mind can be transformative: Making a slave a master. Not a master of materialism alone, but a master of justice and all that accompanies it. Justice that recognizes the unalienable rights of each soul/mind/body to life, liberty, and the pursuit of happiness. Justice that facilitates a truly participatory government where all are heard, acknowledged, and respected. Justice that ensures that all can participate in producing and enjoying the fundamental requirements of life as it is known on the planet today. Justice that ignites and nourishes bright and wholesome ideas that can lead all in the society to ever higher levels of existence in peace.

If not justice, then what? Whatever it may be, Black America must use it to identify the trap door and the related pass code, which will allow us to renew/recondition our minds to evolve methods and tools that deliver true freedom that permits us to breathe. Otherwise, we will always be slaves.

Conclusion

Let us be clear: We have evolved this chapter along the lines of group achievement. That is, Black America is expected to realize freedom and independence from White America as a group. However, if there is one thing that we know about Black Americans, then it is that we often exhibit an acephalous nature. Because many of us are derived from a Yoruba Culture, we often think and act independently. There is no groupthink here. From the outset of our sojourn in North America, there has been a distinct difference between the "House Negro" and the "Field Negro;" and between those who stole away and headed north, and those who chose to remain behind.

It is true that Black America may adopt a unified and overarching position on important and specific topics. For example, we largely agree that anti-Black racism should end. We also agree generally that White Supremacy should be brought to heel, then expunged/obliterated. At the same time, there are many individual and group efforts underway to bring these desired outcomes into view.

But this reality is not unique. There are usually more ways than one to skin a cat, and there are many levels of effort that may be applied to achieve outcomes. In the end and in most cases, group outcomes result from individual efforts. Even in the most personal of space, our religion, we hear about benefitting from the assembly or the congregation. But it turns out that we must each achieve salvation, enlightenment, nirvana alone—individually.

We referred to experiencing a parthenogenesis as a group, and it may occur. However, by its very nature and by definition, parthenogenesis is an individual event in response to a dire need to sustain life under unusual circumstances. We are operating under unusual circumstances: A nation within a nation on the verge of birth. We have a dire need to sustain our life: We must have birth, independence, and an opportunity to breathe freely. But we are likely to have to experience the required parthenogenesis individually—birthing within our individual selves the means to independence and freedom. We will have to act individually to achieve a direly needed joint end.

As we consider Black America's quandary we should never forget that individual participation in the "call and response" brings the entire group to an exhilarating and ecstatic crescendo. Therefore, it is imaginable that our sustained, individual efforts can bring us to the bliss of independence and freedom.

In other words, only each of us can determine the answer to the question: Once a slave, forever a slave? However, we can be certain that our joint answers will direct us either to a paradise in Shabazzland/Zion or lead us to the depths of an American hell.[6]

---

[6] Shabazzland and Zion are two potential names for a new Black American homeland.

Chapter Three: All it Takes Is One

Meditation

This chapter asks and answers the fundamental question that any right-minded Black American should ask: "Can Black America live permanently at peace with White America?" It scours the history of the world to tell the same story over and over again that an effort by Black and White Americans to live together is an untenable and unstable equilibrium. With that answer in hand, the next question is: "What to do?" An obvious answer is to live separate lives. Hence the requirement that Black America exodus from White America.

Please read this chapter carefully to convince yourself that the just-delineated argument is sound. Once you reach that conclusion, then you will be well on your way to starting the exodus journey.

Introduction

Malcolm X is often said to say, "The study of history is sufficient to reward all research." In other words, you will be rewarded if you have studied the history of topics and know them in their totality. Now connect the quote with the fact that humans are unique in their ability to transmit the spoken and written word down the generations. Bringing these two important points together helps us to recognize a key fact of history: Ethnic groups that occupy a common geographical territory and reflect a history of one group exploiting or oppressing the other group naturally find their way to violent conflict—unless there is an escape mechanism. The moral of this historical fact is that, if two ethnic groups fit the just elaborated description, then they should rush to fashion an escape mechanism or prepare for war. Another important fact is that history often shows that there is one incident or one person who sparks the conflict between ethnic groups who have lived the oppressor-oppressed paradigm: hence the title of this essay. Importantly, no matter how long two ethnic groups live in "peace" after experiencing the oppressor-oppressed paradigm, all it takes is for one individual to call forth the memories of the past in order to spark the violent and vicious clashes that characterize these conflicts.

This chapter seeks to explore these historical phenomena in detail. First, we assess the "power of one" in an effort to comprehend how one individual is sufficient to motivate change. We then turn our attention to the multiple historical cases of oppressor-oppressed relationships that ended in violent conflict after periods of "peace." Critically, we find that a key to the avoidance or minimization of conflict is the availability of an escape valve in the form of exodus, partition, or nation formation. We undertake this exercise as a warning to the people of the United States who fit perfectly the oppressor-oppressed paradigm and an extended period of relative peace. History predicts that, at some point in the future, White and Black Americans will experience the type of widespread violent conflict that groups in an oppressor-oppressed relationship have experienced unless they separate beforehand.[7]

---

[7] This is not to say that such violent clashes have not already occurred: e.g., the November 18, 1898 Race Riot in Wilmington, North Carolina; the May 31, 1921 Riot in Tulsa, Oklahoma; the January 1923 Rosewood, Florida Massacre; and other race infused riots that have visited America's major cities at various points during the 20th and 21st centuries.

The Power of One

We are reminded of one of the most powerful examples of the "power of one" when we define ourselves religiously. Buddhist, Judeo-Christian, and Islamic traditions are all built on the concept that one individual was elected out of the mass of available populations to initiate a new message. The Gautama Buddha, Abraham, Jesus, and Muhammad were lone individuals who started world changing religious philosophies using the "power of one." This idea of one individual with a transformative presence is also highlighted in religious literature in the pursuit of one who can set things right and preserve mankind. In the case of the destruction of Sodom and Gomorrah, the question boiled down to, "Is there one righteous man in the city?" The answer was "yes" and he will be spared."[8] In the context of the end of time in the Christian tradition as related in the *Revelations* there is a search for one who is worthy/capable of unsealing the great book. The Lamb is found to be sufficient.[9]

While these examples of the "power of one" are related to producing positive outcomes, history is also replete with examples of the power of one for evil. In the 20th century, the iconic symbol of the "power of one" for evil is Adolf Hitler.

We must add a new category to the "power of one" in addition to good and evil those who use the "power of one" to bring about delayed justice. In the American context, whether we call the names of Gabriel Prosser, Denmark Vesey, Nat Turner, H. Rap Brown, or Stokely Carmichael (aka Kwame Ture), these were individuals who sought to motivate violent action as a way to create long-denied

---

[8] See the 18th and 19th Chapters of *Genesis*, *Holy Bible*.
[9] See the 5th Chapter of *Revelations*, *Holy Bible*.

justice. Although oppressors may characterize these personalities as evil, the oppressed, on the other hand, view them as sparking slave rebellions, civil rights protests, and riots as paths to justice.

Oppressor-oppressed relationships do not always have to end in violent conflict. For example, Mahatma Gandhi, Martin Luther King, and Nelson Mandela used their "power of one" in an effort to resolve ethnically charged situations using a non-violent approach.[10] What history tells us is that, if there is an escape hatch, then two ethnic groups can end their prolonged and tense relationships amicably. We examine the range of possible outcomes for parties in oppressor-oppressed relationships below. But before we engage in that analysis, let us discuss the nature of long-awaited justice.

Long-Awaited Justice

There are many historical occurrences when oppressor-oppressed ethnic groups exist for extended periods in relative peace before action is taken to usher up justice for the oppressed. The classic case from 2,500-to-3,500 years ago is the case of the Hebrews being oppressed by the Egyptians.[11] This biblical story ends with the Hebrews escaping to the "promised land." Conflict is avoided because there was an escape hatch. Otherwise, history would have been written differently. In all likelihood, we would have found that the Hebrews ultimately engaged in violent clashes with the Egyptians. Either the Egyptians would have defeated them, or the Hebrews would have found a way to

---

[10] This chapter does not address non-violent approaches to resolving ethnic-related crises.

[11] We should note that there continues to be a great controversy over whether the so-called Hebrews were ever in Egypt—at least as described in the *Old Testament*.

defeat the Egyptians. In a worst-case scenario, the Egyptians may have been successful in fully absorbing the Hebrews into their society through amalgamation and we would have never known the story of the biblical Jews. In fact, given that Black Americans often identify with the biblical Hebrews, the former face the same possible scenarios as did the latter.

In addition to the Hebrew exodus, below we discuss the following oppressor-oppressed relationships: Hindus-Muslims of India; the Hutus-Tutsis of Rwanda; the Christians-Muslims of Bosnia-Herzegovina; the Sinhalese-Tamils of Sri Lanka; and the Northern-Southern Sudanese. In each case we provide a summary of the conditions that led to conflict. Most importantly, we identify lone individuals who played the most significant role in initiating the conflict or in bringing a just conclusion to the conflict. In each case, we look for the critical "power of one."

Exodus' Hebrews and Egyptians

As the biblical story in Exodus goes, Yahweh calls Moses to lead the children of Israel out of Egypt. He is instructed to go with his brother Aaron to Pharaoh and tell him to "let the people go."[12] Because Pharaoh was benefiting from the oppression of the Israelites, he forbade them to depart. Ultimately, after several rounds of plagues, Pharaoh reluctantly agrees to the request.

You may ask: "Didn't Pharaoh understand that two peoples who experience the oppressor-oppressed paradigm end in violent conflict?" Yes, Pharaoh may have understood this

---

[12] The role of Aaron as a confirmer, augmenter, and helper of the one is often repeated in the stories of those great ones who manufacture change in an oppressor-oppressed paradigm. In fact, in the biblical context, the saying is, "For where two or three are gathered together in my name…" (*Matthew* 18:20, *Holy Bible*).

phenomenon. However, Pharaoh had a plan. He cleverly thought that the Egyptians would absorb the Hebrews into Egyptian society. Remember his command to the midwives to kill the male children?[13] Pharaoh planned to limit the reproductive capacity of the Hebrews, then to take the women and produce his own kind with them. But as the story goes, he did not have a chance to work his plan. The children of Israel escaped across the Red Sea, while Pharaoh and his army drowned.

The key points from this story are that the Egyptians and the Israelites were locked in an oppressor-oppressed relationship, which would likely have ended in violent conflict had it not been for the escape hatch, and that Moses used the "power of one" to effect the liberation of—effect long-delayed justice for—his people.

India's Hindus and Muslims

Beginning with the onset of the Vedic civilization of India and up to around 1100 BCE, Hinduism as a religion formed and pervaded the Indian subcontinent. Over time, that part of the world was subject to infiltration by a variety of cultures and traditions, but Hinduism held sway. It was during this period that higher caste Hindus established themselves as rulers over the lower caste Dalits. After about 700 CE, Islamic sultanates formed in various areas of the subcontinent as Mohammedanism spread its influence. During this period, many Dalits converted to Islam in order to escape the oppression visited upon them by upper-caste Hindus. In 1525, there was a new and powerful incursion of Islamic origin into India that formed the basis of Moghul rule, which dominated the subcontinent until about 1860. However, even during the Moghul era, rulership was tolerant

---

[13] See the 1st Chapter of *Exodus, Holy Bible*.

and amenable to Hinduism. This history allowed sizeable populations of Hindus and Muslims to develop jointly in India.[14]

The British Crown came to rule India in the second half of the 19th century. By the early 20th century, it became clear to certain Muslims that, because of an oppressor-oppressed relationship, Hindus and Muslims should form separate communities. Under the British, and with their support, the Hindus pushed down hard on the Muslim population. The writer/philosopher Allama Iqbal was the first major proponent of such separation. Iqbal, in his 1930 address to the All India Muslim League, called for the formation of a separate Muslim nation.[15] Iqbal's "power of one" drove this idea forward to the 1947 Indian Partition, at which time Muhammad Jinnah led the formation of a Pakistan State.

In the events surrounding the 1947 Partition, from 500,000-to-1 million Muslims and Hindus lost their lives in inter-communal violence as massive numbers of Muslims and Hindus traveled in opposite directions to occupy East and West Pakistan and India.[16] Arguably, even more lives might have been lost over the course of history if the two groups had not chosen to separate at Partition. This argument has great weight given the continued high levels of tension and clashes that have characterized the relationship between Pakistan and India and Hindus and Muslims in India even to

---

[14]Percival Spear. (1972) *India: A Modern History*. University of Michigan Press: Ann Arbor. Stanley Wolpert. (1982) *A New History of India,* Second Edition. Oxford University Press: New York.

[15]Details of Iqbal's life are provided here. https://www.iqbal.com.pk/iqbal/life-of-iqbal; retrieved on November 1, 2020.

[16] Barbara Metcalf and Thomas Metcalf. (2006) *A Concise History of Modern India.* Cambridge University Press: Cambridge. [This estimate of those who lost their lives differs from the estimate given in Chapter 4.]

this day. Clearly, the escape hatch, which minimized loss of life, was Partition. Nevertheless, it was the economics and religious-centric nature of the oppressor-oppressed relationship of the Hindus and Muslims, respectively, which forced Partition, and Iqbal was a key actor in fashioning a life-saving escape hatch.

Rwanda's Tutsis and Hutus

In 1994, the Hutus of Rwanda committed genocide against their fellow Tutsis. Tutsi leaders ignored the escape hatch that was available and initiated an insurgent war that produced the genocide against them. Why? Was justice served? What was the nature of the oppressor-oppressed relationship?

Although the scholar Jan Vansina produced certain evidence that ethnic differences surfaced in Rwanda as early as the 17th century, and that Rwandans were not eternally united prior to the advent of European colonizers, popular history traces Rwanda's ethnic problems to the colonizers.[17] That history argues that the Germans (1890-1916) and Belgians (1918-1962) created and defined ethnicity in Rwanda. First, the colonizers made Tutsi cattle holders to be more highly valued than farming Hutus, while Twa hunters were placed at the bottom of the social hierarchy. The Germans employed the Tutsis to serve as the fulcrum of the former's indirect rule of Rwanda. As a result, Tutsis controlled wealth and positions disproportionate to their population. When the Tutsis leveraged their position to seek independence during the 1950s, the Belgians unearthed the Hamitic immigrant (from Northeast Africa) status of the Tutsis to motivate the Hutus to oppose the Tutsis as controllers of Rwanda. In

---

[17] Jan Vansina. (2004) *The Antecedents of Modern Rwanda: The Nyiginya Kingdom.* University of Wisconsin Press: Madison.

November of 1959, the Hutus rose up against the Tutsis, killing some 1,000 of them and sending a sizeable contingent of Tutsis into exile in Uganda. A key leader of this Hutu movement was Grégoire Kayibanda, who was an important signatory to the "Bahutu Manifesto," which sought to legitimize Hutu's historical right to rule Rwanda. Under the Hutus' leadership, Rwanda gained independence from Belgium in 1962, with Kayibanda serving as president.[18]

In 1972, Kayibanda was replaced by Juvénal Habyarimana in a *coupe d'état*. The latter extended Hutu oppressive practices against Tutsis who remained in the country. Nevertheless, Hutus and Tutsis lived in relative harmony until 1990. At that time, a Rwandan Patriotic Front /Army (RPF/A) of Tutsis rose up in Uganda and poured back into to Rwanda to initiate an insurgent war against the Hutus. Paul Kagame was a key decision maker in this Tutsi effort to claim their right to live respected lives in the Rwandan nation that they had inhabited for centuries.[19] Unfortunately, this insurgency ultimately led to the assassination of President Habyarimana and precipitated the horrific genocide of the Tutsis to which we referred at the outset of this section. From 500,000-to-1 million Rwandans (Tutsis and Hutus) lost their lives during this genocide.

Irrespective of whether all Rwandans lived in peace prior to colonization, or whether the colonizers instigated ethnic conflict, the fact remains that the Tutsi minority had a 1959 escape hatch to leave Rwanda. Out of commitment to justice, they ignored the safety of that escape hatch and sought to force change on Rwanda with the 1990 insurgency. Ultimately, the RPF/A succeeded in forcing change on

---

[18] Susanne Buckley-Zistel. (2009) "Nation, Narration, Unification? The Politics of History Teaching After the Rwanda Genocide," *Journal of Genocide Research*: Vol. 11, No. 1; pp. 31-53.
[19] Ibid.

Rwanda—although at a very high cost. Today, Paul Kagame leads Rwanda in its efforts to place the horrific genocide in the past and to move the nation forward.

The case of the Tutsis and Hutus of Rwanda differs from most cases cited in this chapter because the Tutsis, although a "minority" population-wise, exercised power over the majority—at least at the outset of the story. They were viewed as "oppressors." Many of them were forced out of their homeland, but fought their way back in. Nevertheless, the magnitude of the genocide that occurred in Rwanda will not be lost to history, and it may be difficult to create a future in which Tutsis and Hutus view each other as equals. As long as there is a chance that future Hutus will view themselves as oppressed and the Tutsis as oppressors, then either a new escape hatch will have to be formed for the Tutsis, or we may see renewed rounds of genocidal violence in Rwanda. Importantly, Paul Kagame used the "power of one" to help create conditions under which the Tutsis and Hutus can make an effort to live together in peace in Rwanda today.

Bosnia-Herzegovina's Muslims and Christians

While all hell was breaking loose in Rwanda, a different crisis was unfolding in what we know today as Bosnia-Herzegovina (BH)—a republic in the former Yugoslavia. It is a very complicated story that goes back several hundred years. Nevertheless, we condense the story so that you can witness another case of ethnic groups engaging in genocidal war after living together in relative peace for an extended period.

The Islamic Ottoman Empire came to control what was the former Yugoslavia during the 14th century. It was successful in converting to Islam many Serbians and Croatians who were living in that part of Eastern Europe. The Serbs were

Eastern Orthodox Christians and the Croats were Roman Catholics.[20] Add in newly converted Muslims who are known as Bosniaks and you have an interesting mix of religious ethnicities and a basis for ethnic nationalism.

One cannot argue that there was perfect peace in the region from the 14th to the 19th centuries. However, there was no major genocidal war between the groups on the order of that to be discussed here. Ethnic nationalism began its expression in a pronounced way in the 20th century. Following World War I, the Serbs came to control the territory known as the former Yugoslavia. The Croats, however, pushed back on the Serbs during the 1920s and 1930s because they viewed Serbian rule as brutal. When the German Nazis invaded the territory during World War II, the Croats took the opportunity to establish a fascist regime (the Ustasha), which took vengeance out mainly on the Serbs.[21]

After World War II, Field Marshall Josip Broz Tito established a communist state in the former Yugoslavia with six republics (BH, Serbia, Montenegro, Macedonia, Slovenia, and Croatia) and two autonomous provinces (Vojvodina and Kosovo). He maintained control and kept the nation unified until his passing in 1980. At that time, communism began to lose its grip as the Cold War came to an end. Fearing that the state would fall into disarray, the Serbs accepted Slobodan Milosevic as their leader.[22] Milosevic used his "power of one" to begin to consolidate Serbian power in the former Yugoslavia based on ethnic

---

[20] Brad Joseph. (2005) "Teaching about the Former Yugoslavia." *The Social Studies*. May/June; pp. 133-136.
[21] Ibid.
[22] Center for Balkan Development. (1996) "History of the War in Bosnia: Historical Background." http://www.balkandevelopment.org/edu_bos.html; retrieved on November 1, 2020.

nationalism. However, his rush to consolidate power beyond Serbia over other republics at the national level caused Croatia and BH to seek independence.

Milosevic, who controlled what remained of Yugoslavia's national army (the JNA), attacked Croatia when the latter claimed independence in 1991. That same military would turn on BH when it claimed independence in 1992.

BH was occupied by Bosniaks (44 percent), Serbs (31 percent), and Croats (17 percent). BH used a referendum to decide whether to seek independence. Serbs who supported Milosevic under ethnic nationalism boycotted the referendum. After independence was declared, many BH Serbs took up arms against their fellow Bosniaks and Croats. Because Serbs occupied no specific area of BH, the stage was set for war throughout BH. Under Serbian nationalism, BH Serbs and the JNA began an ethnic cleansing process within BH to establish a purely Serb republic, which could join Serbia under Milosevic's rule.[23] The Serbs were successful in carving out of BH a new republic—the Republika Srpska.

At the same time, under the banner of Croatian nationalism and backed by Croatian forces, BH Croats began their own ethnic cleansing effort against Bosniaks and Serbs to carve out a Croat republic, which could join Croatia under the leadership of President Franjo Tudjman. However, BH Croats and Croatian military forces aligned with BH's army (comprised mainly of Bosniaks) during portions of the conflict to fight BH Serbians and the JNA.[24]

---

[23] Ibid.
[24] United Nations. (2003) "General Findings: Historical Background." *International Tribunal for the Prosecution of Persons Responsible for Serious Violations of International Humanitarian Law Committed in the Territory of Former Yugoslavia since 1991* (pp. 5-9).

The fighting continued until 1995. Due to a United Nations (UN) enforced arms embargo, the Bosniaks were left with limited fighting capabilities. Fortunately, they were able to transform certain factories that they controlled into arms producing units. Nevertheless, they were forced to fight an unwinnable war against the Serbs and, at times, against the Croats. Ultimately, a world outcry against the inhumanity being visited upon the Bosniaks caused UN and North Atlantic Treaty Organization (NATO) forces to enter the region and to help bring the fighting to an end.[25]

Before they could stop the fighting, however, it is estimated that well over 100,000 citizens of BH—most of them Bosniaks—lost their lives. Hundreds of thousands were injured by the fighting. Keep in mind that life for the living was not pleasant. Many Bosniak males and females were placed in concentration camps under horrific conditions and the latter were often raped by Serbs and Croats as an expression of power and control.[26]

This genocidal conflict ended with BH being partitioned into the Republika Srpska (49 percent of the territory) under Serb control and the Federation of BH (51 percent of the territory) under joint control by the Bosniaks and Croats.[27] To cast it in best terms, the UN acted to make sour lemonade out of lemons.

This is a case of the "power of one" (Milosevic) being used to produce very undesirable outcomes: Genocide; the imposition of inhuman conditions mainly upon Bosniaks;

---

http://www.icty.org/x/cases/naletilic_martinovic/tjug/en/nal-tj030331-e.pdf; retrieved on November 1, 2020.
[25] Richard Holbrooke. (1999) *To End a War*. Random House: New York.
[26] Op. cit. (Center for Balkan Development)
[27] Op. cit. (Center for Balkan Development)

and the partition and physical destruction of a country. Unfortunately, no Bosniak rose up with the "power of one" to seek justice successfully for his/her people. Consequently, we should not conclude that the "case is closed." On the contrary, it may very well be that, at some point in the future, Bosniaks will rise up to serve vengeance on their Croat neighbors and on Serbs with whom they now share a border.[28]

Sri Lanka's Sinhalese and Tamils

Arguably, the Sinhalese-Tamil conflict dates back to the arrival of Tamils to the Island of Ceylon (today, Sri Lanka) in the 2nd century BCE because the two groups jockeyed for territory from the outset.[29] On the other hand, one could argue that the conflict originated at the point of independence from the island nation's final colonial master, the British, in 1948. Whatever the starting point, politicization of the two groups' differences by Sinhalese politicians in the 1950s in order to win votes caused Tamils to begin losing faith in the nation's ability to operate democratically and fertilized the seeds of a separatist movement. Fearing relegation to second-class status, Tamils sought self-determination under self-rule.[30]

Although there were periodic frictions, Sinhalese and Tamils lived mainly peaceably together on the island—even under colonial rule (1517-1948). During the 19th century and first half of the 20th century the British used the Tamil minority

---

[28] The nations discussed in this section are discussed further in Chapter 4.
[29] Sinnappah Asaratnam. (1964) *Ceylon*. Prentice-Hall: Englewood Cliffs.
[30] A.R.M. Imtiyaz and Ben Stavis. (2008) "Ethno-Political Conflict in Sri Lanka." *Journal of Third World Studies*. Vol. XXV, No. 2; pp. 135-52.

to administer the former's affairs using the English language in a traditional "divide and conquer" scheme. Therefore, Tamils held key governance positions that they desired to retain. After independence the majority Sinhalese Buddhist gained control of governance and, under the leadership of Prime Minister S.W.R.D. Bandaranaike, sought to solidify that control by formulating a "Sinhala-Only" language policy in 1956. Almost 20 years later in 1972 a new educational standardization policy permitted Sinhalese students to enter science and medicine programs with lower scores than Tamils on admittance exams. Also, in 1972 Sri Lanka's Constitution conferred special status on Buddhism, which was an affront to Tamil Hindus. These ethnically divisive actions caused communal riots to erupt in 1958, 1961, 1974, and 1977 in which Tamils were killed, robbed, maimed, and rendered homeless.[31]

Throughout this period, the Tamils organized and formed many groups that opposed Sinhalese discriminatory acts. After founding the Tamil New Tigers (TNT) in 1972 Velupillai Prabhakaran rose to lead the Liberation Tigers of Tamil Eelam (LTTE)—the most important Tamil group. He shaped the LTTE into a finely tuned organization with military, educational, administrative, financial, diplomatic, and international arms.[32]

In July/August 1983 the Sinhalese began a Tamil ethnic cleansing campaign, which was ostensibly sanctioned by the Government of Sri Lanka (GOSL). The Tamils fought back and started a war that would extend through the spring of 2009. Noted for suicide bombings that killed high-ranking GOSL leaders, the LTTE used all available tactics to impose

---

[31] Ibid.
[32] Rohan Gunaratna. (1997) *International and Regional Implications of the Sri Lankan Tamil Insurgency*. AABC for International Studies: Colombo.

death and suffering on the Sinhalese who comprised an outsized majority. For this ruthless and relentless fighting, much of the world branded the LTTE a "terrorist organization." At the same time, the GOSL permitted its military to act indiscriminately at times inflicting death and suffering on Tamils.[33]

There were numerous attempts to resolve the crisis over the 26 years that it lasted. India contributed its assistance to resolve the problem. European nations, particularly the Norwegians, came to help. After the turn of the millennium a 2002 Cease Fire Agreement (CFA) was negotiated, and peace talks between the GOSL and the LTTE were conducted in key cities around the world. The international community pledged USD 4.5 billion to assist the nation in reorganizing and rebuilding in a way that would permit the LTTE to have certain autonomous rights in a federal governance system.[34] For a variety of complicated reasons, the CFA broke down. By 2006, the two parties were engaged in full-scale war again. Under the leadership of President Mahinda Rajapaksa, who was elected in November of 2005, the GOSL raised defense expenditures dramatically and directed its military to squeeze the LTTE out of the northern and eastern regions of the country.

By 2008 the LTTE was pushed out of its eastern stronghold and concentrated its forces in the northern province of Jaffna. In late 2008 the Sri Lanka military began attacking Jaffna. Ground and air attacks systematically reduced the territory controlled by the LTTE.[35] Civilians were caught in

---

[33] Amita Shastri. (2009) "Ending Ethnic Civil War: The Peace Process in Sri Lanka." *Commonwealth & Comparative Politics*. Vol. 47, No. 1; pp. 76-99.
[34] Ibid.
[35] Somini Sengupta. (2009) "Sri Lanka Captures Rebel Stronghold." *The New York Times*. January 25th.

this squeeze and thousands died and were injured. There were reports of Sri Lankan Air Force bombings of civilian targets on the one hand, and reports of LTTE forcibly conscripting Tamil youth to fight the war on the other. The international community took notice of the bloodbath that was unfolding in northern Sri Lanka.[36] On May 18, 2009 Sri Lanka's defense forces captured the last LTTE positions in Jaffna and the LTTE surrendered. On the 19th of May Prabhakaran was killed along with his top aides as they tried to escape the region in an ambulance.[37] The war was over.

Although Prabhakaran and the LTTE were logical in their pursuit of autonomy, their actions were extremist. They were successful in assassinating key leaders and shocking the world with their violence, but they alienated the world. Moreover, the LTTE's terrorism ultimately motivated the GOSL to initiate an all-out war. That is not to say that the Sri Lankan military was circumspect in all of its actions. This almost endless war in this small island nation got out of control. Expert negotiators were unable to reconcile the parties. Something besides the principles on which the war was started entered the picture—possibly the wealth that war can bring—and took the entire affair off course.

Unlike other oppressor-oppressed ethnic conflicts, the Sri Lankan War had no heroes who used the "power of one" to secure justice and peace. This war produced at least 70,000 dead; tens of thousands wounded; hundreds of thousands

---

http://www.nytimes.com/2009/01/26/world/asia/26lanka.html?scp=1&sq=Sri%20Lankan%20Troops%20Take%20Last%20Rebel%20Stronghold&st=cse; retrieved on November 1, 2020.
[36] BBC News. (2009) "UN Mourns Sri Lankan Bloodbath." May 11th. http://news.bbc.co.uk/2/hi/8043169.stm; retrieved on November 1, 2020.
[37] BBC News. (2009) "Sri Lanka's Rebel Leader Killed." May 19th. http://news.bbc.co.uk/2/hi/8055015.stm; retrieved on November 1, 2020.

homeless; massive amounts of destroyed infrastructure; billions of dollars wasted; and a fractured Tamil society that may rise up to fight the Sinhalese again.

Sudan's North and South

The story of Southern Sudan, too, evolves out of an economic and ethnocentric oppressor-oppressed relationship. The British, under pre-independence control of the territory that is now Sudan, sought to establish two areas: One in the north for Arabs, and one in the south for Zurgas or Blacks.[38] As independence was unfolding in the mid-1950s Sudan was already engulfed in its first north-south civil war, which lasted from 1955 until 1972. In 1972 under the leadership of Lt. Gen. Joseph Lagu Yanga an Addis Abbaba Accord was reached, which called for the establishment of an autonomous region in the south of a newly independent nation of Sudan. That arrangement fared well for nearly a decade. However, in 1983, Sudanese President, Gaafar Nimeiry, nullified the autonomous status of Southern Sudan and declared that Sudan was one nation.[39] This sparked a second civil war, which spanned 1983-2005. While a peace agreement was reached in 2005, ethnic-based (genocidal) atrocities continued in Darfur and elsewhere in the southern portion of the country. Finally, in January 2011, a referendum was conducted in the south and 99 percent of the electorate voted for independence. On July 9, 2011, the

---

[38] Mahmood Mamdani. (2009) "The International Criminal Court's Case Against the President of Sudan: A Critical Look." *Journal of International Affairs*. Vol. 62, No. 2; pp. 85-92.
[39] The European Sudanese Public Affairs Council. "A Chronological History." http://www.espac.org/peace_process/search_for_peace3.asp; retrieved on November 1, 2020.

nation of South Sudan was established formally.[40] Even so, Sudan continued to retaliate against the newly established South Sudan with military attacks. The latter is rich with timber, petroleum, iron ore, copper, chromium, zinc, tungsten, micra, silver, gold, diamonds, hydropower, hardwood, and limestone.

Although there were many important leaders from Southern Sudan over the past 50 years, including founders of the especially important Sudan People Liberation Army and Movement (SPLA/M; Joseph Oduho and John Garang), the most important leader was Joseph Lagu Yanga. He was the first to bring to the attention of the people of Southern Sudan the importance of autonomy to develop, manage, and benefit from their rich mineral and other natural resources.

Therefore, the case of South Sudan brings together elements of economics and ethnic groups (the Arabs of the north (Sudan) and the Black tribal groups of Southern Sudan) to fashion an untenable oppressor-oppressed arrangement that festered through two civil wars. While complete peace remains elusive, at least definitive steps toward peace are possible under the current complete separation of Southern from Northern Sudan. History tells us that hundreds of thousands of lives could have been saved had South Sudan been successful in forming an independent nation after the first civil war. Also, it tells us that Joseph Lagu Yanga's "power of one" was sufficient to drive the vision of nation formation for South Sudan to its ultimate conclusion.

---

[40] Central Intelligence Agency. (2012) "South Sudan: Introduction." *CIA World Factbook.* https://www.cia.gov/library/publications/the-world-factbook/geos/od.html; retrieved on November 1, 2020.

The Best Option

The four stories of the Hebrews and Egyptians, the Hindus and Muslims of India, the Christians and Muslims of Bosnia-Herzegovina, and the Northern and Southern Sudanese reveal a common thread: "It took nation formation to avoid, minimize, or resolve violent conflicts that resulted from oppressor-oppressed ethnic relationships." The remaining two stories (Rwanda and Sri Lanka) that we tell in this chapter concerning wars that ended with oppressor-oppressed groups continuing to occupy the same national space do not have clean and final endings. One can easily imagine that Tutsis and Hutus and the Sinhalese and Tamils may find themselves reengaged in horrendous wars in the future to find an ultimate solution to their historical animosities.

Consequently, our reading of selected history leads us to the conclusion that, if two ethnic groups are locked in an oppressor-oppressed relationship (even when that relationship is an artifact of past history), then the two groups should move toward complete separation through nation formation.[41] If they do not adopt this approach, then there is a high probability that the "power of one" will spark a violent conflict—to superimpose oppression or to secure justice—that could otherwise be avoided.

---

[41] We write "selected history" because we only address selected cases in history. Other important 20th century cases that come to mind are the German-Jewish Holocaust, the clash between Catholics and Protestants in Northern Ireland, and the genocide that occurred in Cambodia. Important but excluded 21st century case involves the Uighurs of China, the Rohingyas of Myanmar, and the multi-ethnic confrontation that is ongoing currently in Ethiopia.

Conclusion

Despite our accelerated march toward greater knowledge, the human race continues to fail to resolve amicably resource distribution issues. This is particularly true in the context of oppressor-oppressed relationships. In other words, although we continue to increase our intellectual sophistication, we continue to forge conditions that result in violent conflict. We are not too civilized to be uncivilized. In fact, today we use every media means at our disposal to spread the gospel of militarization and we increasingly teach ourselves how to fight. We do not take lightly the adage, "prepare for war in times of peace." If you discount the likelihood of violent conflict, then simply talk to the survivors of recent genocidal conflicts. They, too, had no inkling that they could become the target of massive violence seemingly overnight.

Therefore, it is almost inevitable that two groups that are brought together through history in an oppressor-oppressed relationship will ultimately clash in violent conflict. At some point, the "majority" group may look for a way to incite the violence, because it fears the "minority" group will find a critical weakness and exploit it. Conversely, the minority (out) group fears that it will be locked in a subservient role forever and may seek to turn the table. Whatever the rationale, it is logical to expect violent conflict in this scenario. This chapter sought to show that the way to avoid such conflict is for the two groups to separate under a mutually agreeable arrangement. If they do not, then they only delay the day when conflict comes and/or they ensure extended rounds of violent conflict.

Also, this chapter sought to show that "all it takes is one:" One individual to extend oppression or to liberate the oppressed. In the American context every time we see one more Black male or female incarcerated, murdered in the street, or aborted we know that we may have lost an important "power of one."

Given that White America does not seem to take seriously the potential for conflict within its borders (or dismisses the idea because of its police powers) Black Americans must take it upon ourselves to secure our future by opting for nation formation. If we do not, then we guarantee future violent conflict. If conflict is in the offing, then we only hope that the one who sparks the conflict is a Black supreme strategist.

Chapter Four: Nation Formation Through Migration

Introduction

This brief chapter conveys that nations have formed in the past and are being formed all the time through migrations. We explore the concept of nation formation through emigration and immigration from a variety of angles, including sharing recent statistics from the United Nations (UN) that characterize this process. The main purpose in undertaking this analysis is to show that Black Americans can embark upon nation formation by emigrating from our current locations in the US to other state-wise locations or by becoming immigrants to Shabazzland/Zion, a territory established in the US for occupation by Black Americans.[42]

We provide a foundation for the concept of nation formation through migration using a well-known fact: In modern world history the formation of North, Central, and South American nations rests on migration and slavery. We follow that up with a discussion of the fact that hundreds of millions of people are migrating each year to new nations. We highlight the fact that the most recently formed nations have not relied on immigration to any great extent. We discuss that many nations today, even though they were formed many years ago, have a high percentage of immigrants in their populations. Finally, we conclude the chapter by exploring a case that parallels in many ways the expected path of Black America going forward—especially in the event of an exodus. That is, we recall India's Partition, which was discussed in Chapter Three.

---

[42] Again, Shabazzland/Zion are names that we have proposed for a Black American homeland.

North, Central, and South American Nation Formation

It is common knowledge that, while Christopher Columbus did not "discover" America, his voyages to the Americas in the late 15th century opened a door to exploration primarily by Spanish, French, and British explorers who claimed large territories for the kings and queens of their native lands.[43] This sparked a wave of migrations to what we know today as North, Central, and South American lands by populations from these European countries. Once the African Slave Trade facilitated free labor that could produce wonderful new crops, goods, and services for consumption in the Americas, in Europe, Africa, and elsewhere, more and more Europeans came to the Americas to seek their fortunes. This started the development process in the Americas in earnest and the rest is history. This is a prime and pertinent example of nation formation through migration. It should be a reminder to Black Americans that migration is a very normal course of action in response to a variety of possible motivating factors. In our case, we should be willing to become immigrants in new American territories in order to achieve freedom and independence—a place to breathe free, heal ourselves, and identify and rise to our true purposes on the world's stage.

Emigration Today

The UN Population Division's Department of Economic and Social Affairs reports that 272 million persons migrated during 2019, which represented about 3.5 percent of the

---

[43] Admittedly, we are ignoring here the history of early North American exploration by adventurers from the northern most parts of Europe. It also ignores the fact that Africans and Asians had engaged in even earlier explorations of the Americas.

world's global population of about 7.7 billion.[44] The world's migration flow is generally increasing as we go forward in history, and migration is likely to represent the primary source of population growth for selected countries in the near future. Which countries represent the largest emigration flows? Table 1 shows the top ten countries and the US, which ranks number 21 in the world.

Table 1.—Top 10 Emigrant Countries of Origin and the US

No.	Emigrant Country of Origin	Number of Emigrants (2019)
1	India	17,510,931
2	Mexico	11,796,178
3	China	10,732,281
4	Russian Federation	10,491,715
5	Syrian Arab Republic	8,225,499
6	Bangladesh	7,835,152
7	Pakistan	6,303,286
8	Ukraine	5,901,067
9	Philippines	5,377,337
10	Afghanistan	5,120,756
21	United States	3,167,072

Source: United Nations and the author

The data show that emerging market and low-income countries with large populations comprise an important source of migrants. But even a country as well-off as the US

---

[44] See United Nations. (2019) "International Migrant Stock: Ten Key Messages." https://www.un.org/en/development/desa/population/migration/publications/migrationreport/docs/MigrationStock2019_TenKeyFindings.pdf; retrieved on October 31, 2020.

is an important source of migrants. While there are no widely-known and high-quality published data sources on the number of Black Americans who emigrate from the US, anecdotal evidence is that the number is increasing as Black Americans seek an improved quality of life outside of the country. Again, the data presented in Table 1 and this section of the chapter are intended to convey that migration is not uncommon, and to suggest that Black Americans should be willing to choose migration as a way to resolve our quandary of living in a racist America.

Recent Nation Formation and Immigration

Since the onset of the 21st century only five new nations have come to the world's stage: Timor Leste (2002); Montenegro (2006); Serbia (2006); Kosovo (2008); and South Sudan (2010).[45] All of these countries have relatively small populations—South Sudan being the largest with a population of about 11 million in 2020. Each of these nations was formed out of conflict, but the conflicts did not produce circumstances in which nation formation occurred through significant migration. In other words, the formation of these five nations mainly involved residents securing the right to govern themselves. We bring these points forward just to emphasize that new nation formation does not have to transpire solely through migration.

Immigrants in Nations' Populations Today

We return now to UN data to make certain important points concerning nation formation and migration. We made the point above that the Americas represent a prime example of nation formation through migration. It is well known that the

---

[45] We discuss Montenegro, Serbia, Kosovo, and South Sudan in Chapter 3.

US has long been a valued destination for immigrants from all over the world. Therefore, Table 2 should not present any startling results.

Table 2.—Top 10 Countries with Stocks of Immigrants by Size

No.	Countries	Migrant Stock in 2019
1	United States	50,661,149
2	Germany	13,132,146
3	Saudi Arabia	13,122,338
4	Russian Federation	11,640,559
5	United Kingdom	9,552,110
6	United Arab Emirates	8,587,256
7	France	8,334,875
8	Canada	7,960,657
9	Australia	7,549,270
10	Italy	6,273,722

Source: United Nations and the author

Table 2 shows the top 10 countries by their immigrant population size. Unsurprisingly, the US has, by far, the world's largest immigrant population. Other developed countries are high on the list, along with a couple of wealthy oil producing countries that draw immigrants to help build infrastructure and to produce goods and services for their native populations.

The US's immigrant population is large and, in the main, immigrants are welcomed very warmly into the American society (often, they are designated as White) and given great assistance, support, and advantages. What is distressing about the latter point is that at the same time that immigrants are being welcomed so warmly into the country, a sizeable proportion of the native Black American population languishes in poverty and despair. There is something wrong with this picture, which has been repeated ad infinitum throughout the course of US history. Simply put, immigration is a "good thing" for those arriving in the US. Black America should seek to make emigration a "good thing" as we migrate to independent living spaces in the US.

India's Partition and Black American Nation Formation

In Chapter 3, we mentioned the primary reason for India's Partition: India's Hindus and Muslims concluded that they could not coexist peaceably in South Asia after independence was secured from Britain (the United Kingdom). Logistically, Partition involved the separation of many of India's Muslims who ventured off to territories that became East and West Pakistan, while many Indian Hindus who were resident of those territories migrated to what is India today.

In an August 10, 2017 article in *The Conversation,* Professor Sarah Ansari describes how India's Partition unfolded.[46] The underlying story is that Muslims represented a sizeable (25 percent) minority in British India and enjoyed important protections. As Britain neared a decision to extend independence to India after World War II, the Muslims feared that their protections would be lost in a Hindu-controlled nation. Therefore, several proposals were lofted concerning Muslim versus Hindu territories that should be created for the two religious groups after independence. While these territorial proposals were aired, little was done

---

[46] Sarah Ansari. (2017) "How the Partition of India Happened—And Why Its Effects are Still Felt Today." *The Conversation.* August 10th. https://theconversation.com/how-the-partition-of-india-happened-and-why-its-effects-are-still-felt-today-81766; retrieved on October 31, 2020.

to plan the logistics of relocating Muslims from predominantly Hindu territories and Hindus from predominantly Muslim territories, or to plan to meet the needs of these newly located populations. Without sound planning, the relocation of millions promised to be a nightmare and it was. We now turn to how Partition unfolded.

In 1946, following great pressure from India's native population, the British Parliament set June 1948 as the deadline for Indian Independence. After a key effort failed to finalize agreement between Hindus and Muslims living in India and the British Government in 1946, Lord Louis Mountbatten arrived in India as a new British Viceroy in March of 1947. He had a mandate to finalize plans for India's independence with all haste. After just over two months, on June 3, Mountbatten announced that independence would be advanced from June 1948 to August 1947. Independence was declared on August 14 by East and West Pakistan and on August 15 by India, 1947. Importantly, and an indicator of the rush to independence, the boundaries that delineated the new nations were not finalized until August 17, 1947.

This haste to resolve an independence problem produced a humanitarian crisis as Muslims shifted from India to the Pakistans and as Hindus shifted from the Pakistans to India. From 14-to-16 million persons relocated during Partition. Because of fear, long-held hatreds, and the anguish of relocating, from 200,000-to-two million persons were killed as human herds crossed paths on their way to new homes. Vidhi Doshi and Nisan Mehdi feature horrific first-hand accounts of Partition in an August 2017 article in the *Washington Post,* and they cause one to conclude that such a crisis could likely have been avoided had more time been allotted to plan Partition.[47]

For Black Americans, there are important takeaways from India's Partition. A key takeaway is that our efforts to migrate in search of freedom and independence are likely to parallel India's Partition for at least three reasons. First, the territories that we will migrate to occupy in the US will likely include White residents who will have to decide to depart or remain; this will generate a two-way traffic flow as in the Indian Partition case. Second, the long-standing animus between Muslims and Hindus parallels the long-standing animus between American Blacks and Whites. And third, at the point of migration or exodus, not all Black Americans will choose to depart for Shabazzland/Zion just as many Muslims remained in India after Partition.

However, the most important takeaway, which has already been alluded to, is that a close reading of Partition's history reveals that much of the nightmare could have been avoided if there had been sufficient foresight to, or sufficient time to, plan Partition. As you move forward to Chapters 5 and 6, you will find a heavy emphasis on planning. Not only planning the politics, economics, and sociology of nation formation through migration, but also logistical planning. Specifically, in Chapter 6 we discuss a phased approach to occupying Shabazzland/Zion—Black America's new nation. Such a phased approach should help to minimize the type of logistical nightmare that was Partition.

---

[47] Vidhi Doshi and Nisan Mehdi. (2017) "70 Years Later—Survivors Recall the Horror of India-Pakistan Partition." *Washington Post.* August 14th. https://www.washingtonpost.com/world/asia-pacific/70-years-later-survivors-recall-the-horrors-of-india-pakistan-partition/2017/08/14/3b8c58e4-7de9-11e7-9026-4a0a64977c92_story.html; retrieved on October 31, 2020.

Conclusion

This brief chapter emphasizes the role of migration in nation formation. While recent nation formation has not counted on migration in large measure, the history of the world is replete with cases of nation formation through migration. Importantly, we should never forget that we live in a nation that has the world's largest population of immigrants. Sadly, those immigrants generally surpass Black Americans in income and wealth shortly after their arrival because of the assistance, support, and privileges that they receive from the nation. Indeed, the need for exodus is rooted in this type of maltreatment of Black Americans by the nation historically.

Now we must flip immigration on its head and emigrate to our preferred locations for freedom and independence. If there are about 272 million annual emigrants in the world today, then certainly Black America can relocate as many of our nearly 45 million as desire to go to new locations in the US. If we achieve freedom and independence through land grabs of sparsely populated states, then the migration burden will be light. If, on the other hand, conditions permit wider spread nation formation, then migration will be more burdensome. However, our knowledge of history will ensure that we do not allow our migration to Shabazzland/Zion to devolve into an Indian Partition. We have the expertise to ensure that our exodus to freedom and independence is quite orderly, peaceful, and successful.

Chapter Five: Future Black Independent Living in the US

Introduction

Imagine that Black Americans developed a *Takeconomics* strategy.[48] That is, in response to our unjust historical experiences in the US, we decided to not await reparations or any other form of recompense that might or might not be forthcoming from the government or non-Black people of the US. Rather, we decided to systematically occupy and take control of territories in which to organize life as we desire. Which territories should be occupied? What would be favorable characteristics/aspects of the territories? Besides the demographic, geological/topographical, and economic characteristics of the territories, are there other important considerations that should be made?

To be honest, to make a perfect decision about which territories to occupy requires extensive study of many potential territories. A key factor in determining which territories to occupy requires considerable knowledge about the people who are going to occupy the territories. Finally, this type of exploratory analysis is inevitably underpinned by certain assumptions. All of these elements need to be laid on the table and considered seriously before a final decision is made.

For a variety of reasons, this analysis will not present a definitive set of prescriptive actions that will lead to successful occupations of territories. However, we want to take this thought experiment to certain logical conclusions that might be useful to those who ultimately entertain the

---

[48] Brooks Robinson. (2019) *Takeconomics: A Counterintuitive Perspective.* BlackEconomics.org: Honolulu.

idea and perform the final analysis so that a decision can be made.

We begin with assumptions, and then move on to the other required considerations in logical sequence. Keep in mind that, even though the details are not given in the literature, Moses, Aaron, and the Israelites had plenty of time to formulate plans to take the "promised land."

Assumptions

The primary assumption is that the government and non-Black people of the US will not extend reparative justice to Black Americans. Accordingly, Black Americans will become increasingly inclined to adopt a *Takeconomics* attitude—i.e., to take what is rightfully ours. Clearly, White America should award to us some of what we helped them get. However, when they fail to do what is just, then we decide to take matters into our own hands.

A second and especially important assumption is that non-Black Americans will be consistent about acting out their racist tendencies. In this case, when we move in, they move out. Specifically, when Black Americans decide on a strategic territory to occupy that territory will, undoubtedly, be occupied already by non-Black Americans. However, given non-Black Americans' racist attitudes, they will make an effort to exit the territory once we begin to move in. In addition, we will have essentially no concern about White Americans outside of the territory clamoring to come in to restore a favorable population balance for Whites once we begin to pour in.

Assumptions that go without saying include: (i) Black Americans will be willing to endure certain potential hardships "for the cause" as part of this territory grabbing process; (ii) when territories are occupied initially they will remain under the jurisdiction of the US Government and will, therefore, receive the economic benefits associated with being part of the US; (iii) our territorial grabbing strategy will be timed so that a US census is taken soon after the grab is complete so that we reap the political and economic benefits that accrue nearly immediately; and (iv) Black Americans who plan to participate in this territorial grabbing strategy will engage in an intensive saving program leading up to execution of the strategy—including being willing to sell any nonfinancial and financial assets that they own, if necessary, so that they have sufficient liquid financial capital to purchase new residential or business properties in the territories to which they migrate. This is not withstanding prospects for absorbing available nonfinancial assets on a no-cost basis.

A final and particularly important assumption that must prove to be true if this territorial grabbing strategy is to be successful is that one can pour new wine into new skins. By this we mean that, although Black Americans may not undergo a formal transformation (educational, religious, etc.) before executing the territorial grabbing strategy, the very decision to take unilateral and purposeful action on our own behalf is indicative of a renewal that makes us new wine. The new skins, of course, are the new environments in which we will find ourselves in the taken territories. If we are to be successful in the territories, then we must walk a new walk, talk a new talk, and come with a new act. We will have new freedoms that mean new responsibilities. We must come to the territories with a deep sense of honor and respect for each other—an overwhelming sense of "community." We must be willing to think, plan, work, love, and fight for one another in ways that we have not for a very long time, and we must cherish the opportunities to do so.

Precursor Considerations

At the forefront of this territorial grab strategy is the idea that we will be taking land that will be owned/controlled by Black Americans far into the future. Our minds must be anchored to the idea that we are not going back to Africa, the Caribbean, or to any part of the US on a permanent basis, other than to areas also owned/controlled by Black Americans. We must be conclusive in this determination knowing that non-Black America had an opportunity to welcome us with open and just arms for 430 years, but failed to do so. The very nature of non-Black Americans during this nearly half of one millennium period was evil.[49] It is no longer just about the past: Each day non-Black Americans are generating more reasons why we should never trust, respect, or want to be associated with them. We certainly should not continue imploring them to permit us to be a part of their society. History speaks for itself, and we need not belabor the point here. The point that must be clear in our minds is that we take this territory for the purpose of meeting our essential needs, including: (1) The right to control our own land or homeland; (2) the need for a refuge in which to grow whole again; and (3) the need to possess a place and space for our generations to come to reside.

As we lean forward into the future of the world, we must be cognizant of the types of developments that may occur and anticipate requirements to respond to those developments. The territory that is taken must have the capacity to meet our basic needs and to accommodate the type of economic system that we are likely to forge. We need to place all of our wise scientists to the task of envisioning the future.

---

[49] Even the elections of Barack Obama as president and Kamala Harris as vice-president embody trickery because neither of them is, in fact, the direct descendant of a so-called Black American slave.

However, we know fundamentally that we must have food and drink, clothing, and shelter. That is, we must be certain that the lands that we take have and will have enough water to grow our crops and to produce the food that we require. The lands should enable us to produce our own clothing and shelter, or goods that we can exchange to acquire the required clothing and shelter. Consequently, the territories that we intend to take must be considered in a long futuristic context to ensure that they will not just meet our short-term requirements, but requirements that are likely to arise far into the future. At the same time, let us realize that: "With food, clothing, and shelter, therewith be contented."

To anyone with eyes and ears open during the past two decades, "Global Warming" and "Sea Level Rise" come to mind as current and/or future conditions that should be accounted for when selecting territories. The literature indicates that the southern latitudes of the US are going to become increasingly warm and dry as global warming materializes. Accordingly, Black Americans should consider moving away from that part of the US. A countervailing opinion is that warmer climates give rise to abundant and cheap solar energy, which can produce fresh water from the sea (desalinization) cheaply. Therefore, we should not reject out-of-hand grabbing territories in the south. Also, the "Climate Change" literature places northern US latitudes in the future favorable zone—i.e., northern latitudes should experience warmer temperatures in comparison to the present, and many northern areas have significant exposure to Great Lakes waters and to waters from melting glaciers existing currently in Canada. In addition, if what is now Canada becomes the ideal place to live far into the future, we would be closer to that territory if our starting point is the northern versus the southern US latitudes. Again, our scientists will have to assist us in assessing the territories to grab.

Another popular argument that should be allowed to influence decisions on territorial locations is that Black Americans might benefit greatly from finding ourselves in completely new surroundings—culturally, geographically, and climatologically. We have been in a house of horrors and in an abusive relationship. Should we not escape that house and the relationship for renewal in a new environment? It may make it easier for us to throw off unhealthy habits and behaviors, and to begin to live wholesome and healthy lives. If this is true, then we should not be afraid to look far and wide for territories to grab as our new home.

Choosing Territories

By territories, we mainly mean states—although we could also mean large portions of states that could be transformed into new and independent states. It is well known that Black Americans have proposed in the past to take control of states in the southern part of the US. In our view, these proposals may be somewhat misguided. We base this conclusion on simple mathematics. Of course, the territorial grab strategy that we are proposing involves much more than simple mathematics. Nevertheless, consider Table 3.

Table 3.—High Black Population Percentage States

No.	States	Black Population Percentage (2010 Estimate)	Estimated White over Black Population Advantage in 2018
1	Georgia	31.5%	3,886,804
2	Louisiana	32.8%	1,603,158
3	Maryland	30.9%	2,308,587
4	Mississippi	37.6%	740,464

Source: US Census Bureau and the author's estimates.

Table 3 informs us that there are four states where the Black population exceeds 30 percent of the total. However, in an attempted territorial grab, it would take a minimum of about a two million Black American migration just to achieve parity with the White population in these states (except for Mississippi), which is insufficient to swamp the White population and enforce control. This ignores the unsound logic of infiltrating some of these states and creating severally strained conditions due to their small physical size.

Now consider Table 4, which shows states where it would take less than two million Black Americans to swamp the White population and take complete control.

Table 4.—States that Black Americans Could Control with a Two Million or Less Black American Migration

No.	States	Estimated White over Black Population Advantage in 2018	Estimated Vacant Housing Units in 2019*
1	Delaware	523,569	36,621
2	Montana	1,045,305	76,177
3	North Dakota	735,021	56,629
4	Rhode Island	901,106	43,744
5	South Dakota	850,367	30,018
6	Vermont	607,596	80,586
7	Wyoming	562,802	41,993

Source: The author's estimates from US Census Bureau statistics.
*--Based on the assumption that 2.5 persons occupy each existing housing unit in the states.

Table 4 tells us that there are seven states (besides Mississippi) where Whites have less than about a one million advantage in population over Black Americans. A two million Black population migration would swamp the existing White population and place Blacks in full control of all of these states. A migration of just a little over one million (about two percent of the nearly 45 million Black Americans) would place all the states under Black American control. Control might be established with smaller migrations if Whites adopt their typical racist practice and take flight when a sizeable Black population appears. Certain Black American religious groups could motivate such a migration alone. Table 4 also shows that, based on our estimates, there are potentially significant housing vacancies that might be used to accommodate a large influx of Black residents—although a considerable amount of new housing would have to be constructed if Whites do not exit. Notably, while a few of these states are very constrained in geographical size, several represent vast territories.

The point on housing availability is very instructive in that, as decisions are being made concerning which territories to grab, significant attention should be paid to housing availability and to how Blacks are to be accommodated shelter-wise once in the new territories.

During the territorial grab decision-making process, significant attention should also be directed at the types of natural resources resident in the states. In addition to water, which we have already mentioned, timber, fisheries, flora and fauna, minerals and ores, and navigable harbors should be assessed. Obviously, the more natural resources available the better the prospect of surviving and flourishing in these territories.

Another set of criteria which should be evaluated by the decision-makers include:

- The topography of the territories: e.g., mountain ranges, hills, grasslands for grazing, farmland for

- agricultural production, and rivers and lakes to support fisheries.
- The extensiveness of the existing road network (paved, dirt roads, and trails) is another important variable.
- The number of bridges should be inversely related to the prospect of selection because it is somewhat difficult and expensive to upkeep bridges. Failure to maintain the bridges could result in disruptions in the flow of people and commerce between important areas within the territories.
- A decision to select territories should be positively correlated with the average age of the existing population. The older the population, the sooner aged Whites will disappear from the landscape, and there is a reduced probability that a small younger population will fight the incursion of Black Americans into the territories.

The territorial grab decision-making process can be conducted largely by the numbers with respect to the above-cited criteria. There are undoubtedly other criteria that will be considered. However, what appears logical is that in America, even in the best of times, well over one million Black Americans remain out of work. We know that many unemployed Black Americans fall into the older age ranges, as do many who are not accounted for in the official statistics. Why cannot a sizeable segment of these Black Americans "sacrifice" and, especially with little or nothing to lose, shift their location and participate in a territorial land grab. We recognize that many may not be able to shift due to their linkage to the criminal justice system. But those who can should shift and rely on the good graces of the US Government to serve as a "safety net" until more Blacks show up, take control, and organize a new life for us in the new territory. This would be a sacrifice well worth it: Laying down one's life to give new life to our posterity.

We need to be strategic, make decisions, and then act swiftly before White America can react. They cannot protect all of the potential territories that we might plan to grab. We can take one state, await White America's response, then take a second territory that is outside of White America's ability to respond and that falls within our strategic plan. We can continue this process until we have enough territory to meet our current and future needs.

Selecting a Territory to Grab

Why not perform at least a preliminary analysis to determine which territory Black Americans should grab? We performed such an analysis and provide details in a set of appendices to this chapter. Starting with the states listed in Table 4 above, we eliminated three states (Delaware, Vermont, and Rhode Island) because their geographic sizes are too small to accommodate a significant portion of Black America's nearly 45 million population individually. Our analysis concerns the remaining four states: Montana, North Dakota, South Dakota, and Wyoming. We collected a range of statistics for 24 fundamental "migration" variables that should be considered when making a long-term decision concerning territories to grab.[50]

Consider the following appendices:

- Appendix A.—A list of the 24 fundamental migration variables and their interpretations.

---

[50] Navigable harbors are excluded from the 24 migration variables because none of the four states under consideration have such harbors.

- Appendix B.—Sources from which statistics on the migration variables were derived.
- Appendix C.—A summary of the migration statistics collected for the four states.
- Appendix D.—A ranking of the states' unweighted migration variables as interpreted.

The ranking noted in Appendix D enabled the formation of a state-wise index, which appears in Table 5. Table 5 shows the incidence of states achieving first (#1s), second (# 2s), third (# 3s), and fourth (# 4s) place rankings with respect to the 24 migration variables.[51] The table shows that Montana is the highest ranked state, followed by North Dakota, Wyoming, and South Dakota. As indicated, this analysis is preliminary in nature, but it proxies for the type of analysis that should be performed and expanded when arriving at a decision on states to target for a territorial grab.

Table 5.—A State-Wise Index of Ranked Migration Variables

Rankings	Wyoming	South Dakota	North Dakota	Montana
# 1s	7	2	6	13
# 2s	7	9	7	3
# 3s	0	10	5	7
# 4s	10	3	6	1
Total Index Value	59	58	61	76

Source: The author using source data (see appendices)

---

[51] Four points were assigned for first place rankings; three points for second place rankings; two points for third place rankings; and one point for fourth place rankings.

The Economy of the Territories

As we contemplate how to operationalize our existence in newly grabbed territories, we need to imagine an economy that is not too complicated, but that utilizes and optimizes the resources that are available—mainly our human capital resources. In a word, we need to build an economy that is composed nearly completely of service industries—the exception being goods producing industries that provide for our physical survival. Simply put, we should build an economy that exists and flourishes simply because we provide goods and services for and to ourselves. Any over production, which might be traded, would be icing on the cake.

In the territories that we occupy initially there will be only a few million persons. The key ingredient to success is to retain a laser-like focus on Black nationalism (Black Power); i.e., to support Black efforts of all types at all costs—to the exclusion of all other groups to the maximum extent possible. This is what White America has done historically and made itself successful in the process (White Power).

There is one precaution about which we should be very cognizant. We must preclude the arising of corruption. Where it does raise its ugly head, we should fight it like the plague. Why? Because corruption is evil and creates animus. Also, it is a wasteful process. As a result, it generates inefficiencies that thwart the generation of goods and services that can add to the quality of life of our people.

Now to the development of a service-oriented economy. We will invert Say's Law and conclude that "demand gets its own supply." Clearly, the millions of Black Americans, who will comprise the economies of the territories, will have certain demands. We will respond to that demand by producing the required supply. We will begin with the production of the three sets of goods that are required for survival, then move on to the services that can be produced.

Agriculture

Keeping it simple we should emphasize to Black Americans in the territories that, until sufficient production is in place to meet demand regularly, each household should perform gardening and produce food for own consumption. In urban areas our governing system should advocate for, and promote the development of, aquaponic-type food production that has been popularized by Mr. Will Allen.[52] This is a year-around cultivation process that is unaffected by climate. Finally, we should motivate and support industrial farming.

To ensure that our food needs are met, we should consider a change in culture and stimulate the onset of mainly vegetarianism. As we know, meat production is an expensive undertaking—the value of which is questionable. Consequently, we should reorient our appetites and reduce our consumption of meat. As exceptions, we may consider the raising of poultry and cattle for egg and milk production, respectively. Our food scientists can provide guidance on diets that ensure good health and longevity. Retail food service will undoubtedly play a role in food supply. However, we should ensure that restaurants that are licensed in the territories produce food that engenders good health.

---

[52] Through his nonprofit organization Growing Power, Mr. Allen promulgated a sustainable model for producing high-quality foods in urban environments. See "Growing Power – A Model for Urban Agriculture. https://www.youtube.com/watch?v=vs7BG4lH3m4; retrieved on November 8, 2020.

Housing

As already noted, territorial selection should be based, in part, on the supply of vacant housing. In other words, the expectation is that for certain territories the need to construct new housing units will be constrained somewhat by the existence of already available housing units. However, undoubtedly, some new housing units will have to be constructed. Our ability to construct required housing units will depend on the skills embodied in the populations that migrate to the territories. To the extent possible, we should try to meet our housing needs with existing labor—even if the quality of housing does not meet expected standards initially. Poor-quality housing can be replaced at a later point when the skill inventory increases/improves. In other words, we should be as self-reliant as possible. Barring an ability to produce housing for ourselves we should import fabricated housing units which we can assemble ourselves—given adequate training. In a worse-case-scenario we can import construction firms to produce housing on our behalf. We should remember that, if American settlers could produce housing from the natural environment with their bare hands, then we should be able to perform at least to that standard.

Electric and Water Utilities

These are critical requirements for our survival. Therefore, we should begin today to convince young Black American girls and boys to enter these industries. When we assume control of the territories these engineers of tomorrow can play significant roles in ensuring our comfort. At the same time, as we know, the territories that we will occupy will already include electric and water utility operations. A large part of the task will be to maintain existing systems and to expand their operations. Obviously, we can learn quickly how to operate existing systems easily. However, it will take special skills to expand the systems from their initial size. This is where our engineers must step in and lead the way. However, if we find that we are lacking skills to operate or expand our electric and water utility systems, then we should seek assistance from other Black and Brown nations of the world. The last thing that we should do is to enlist the help of our former White masters to operate our electric and water systems. If they do, then they will have our lives in their hands again.

A critical aspect of providing electric power is the energy required to run the electricity generating turbines. It is highly likely that most of the electric utility systems will operate using refined carbon-based fuels. If this is the case, then we may have little choice initially other than to import these fuels from White America. However, as a top priority, we should direct our scientists and engineers to seek to remedy this condition as soon as possible by transitioning to other energy forms: Hydro, solar, thermal, wind, etc.

Public Administration Services

If we occupy territories and dominate the demography, then should we not also dominate public administration? In part, this is a political issue because many public officials are elected. However, if we remain true to our Black nationalism, then our votes will carry the day and place Black officials in most, if not all, elected positions. We will control US Senatorial and House of Representatives seats, governorships, state legislatures, county supervisors' positions, and city council positions. By extension, we will head public departments at the state, county, and local levels. We should have complete control of public administration. For the first time in the history of America Black Americans will control the entire gamut of public administration operations in state territories. This is what we can achieve if we operationalize the strategy proposed in this chapter.

Educational Services

Since the onset of integration plans in America in the 1960s, certain Black Americans have complained about busing, about the closure of formerly all-Black schools, about the firing of Black educators, and. most importantly, about the educational performance of Black youth. Under this strategy we have an opportunity to put most, if not all, of these complaints to rest. In the territories that we occupy we will have control of the funding that must be made available by the US Government Department of Education and by ourselves as local taxpayers to ensure that the educational system works for us. This applies not only at the elementary and secondary levels, but at the tertiary level also. Our people will comprise the administrators and superintendents of education, the principals, the professors/teachers, the dieticians, and the custodians in the education system. Black Americans have always valued education. We will value it even more when we are fully responsible for educational outcomes. If the system fails, then we can only point a finger at ourselves.

Health Services

By design, there has been a dearth of Black American health practitioners. We can change all of this in the newly taken territories. Doctors, nurses, and pharmacists that join the migration can take over medical centers, hospitals, and drug counters to ensure that our illnesses are treated properly, and we do not have to worry about doctors or nurses sticking a needle into the brains of our children shortly after birth to cause a retardation of their growth. Black medicine workers can deliver our babies in a safe and secure environment, cure our colds, sew up our cuts, heal our broken bones, and ease our pain. However, given that there will be so few such workers in the beginning, we should make their jobs easier by ensuring that we always exhibit correct behaviors that will keep us out of harm's way—medically. We must take care to eat the correct foods, perform the correct exercise, and avoid stress because we will be "living while Black" in a Black, not White, controlled territory. As we become familiar with our surroundings in the new territory and learn about the plants and herbs that grow there, then we can begin to venture back to some of the old African traditions of finding natural remedies, which may produce better results than some of the modern treatments. This will also reduce our healthcare costs. Importantly, just the reduction in the stress level caused by our arrival and tenure in the newly Black American controlled territory will improve our health and living conditions tremendously. Importantly, we can open the door to many who want to engage in providing healthcare by facilitating training in the field by those who are experts already.

Transportation Services

We may arrive by train, bus, van, car, or motorcycle. Let us all come and bring our modes of transport. Hopefully, we will own these machines outright. Like the Cubans, we have ingenious mechanics who can keep this equipment operating for 30, 40, or 50 years—if need be. In the interim, perhaps we will perfect electric modes of transportation, powered by solar energy.

Once we assume control of the territories, it may be the case that Amtrak, Greyhound, and Trailways will stop coming our way. Not to worry. Black Americans have always had a fascination with automobiles. It could be the result of the fact that travel on an open road was the only real feeling of freedom that we could enjoy—although ever so fleeting until being stopped by a White highway patrolman or reaching the next town. At the same time, we remember Montgomery where we organized a patchwork of taxi services to meet our transportation needs during the great bus boycott. We can repeat this phenomenon in the territories. Forget Amtrak, Greyhound, and Trailways! We can find our own way around our territories. We will coddle the vehicles to make them run; and when they stop, we will cannibalize those that stop to repair those that are still willing to run. However, a key concern is obtaining gasoline on which to run these vehicles. If the territories have natural gas, then maybe we can convert the vehicles to operate on natural gas. Otherwise, we can grow corn and produce ethanol on which to run the vehicles. We will find a way to meet our transportation needs—barring being held hostage to gasoline imported from the US. If push comes to shove, then we can always revert to older forms of transportation until we can leapfrog to the electric vehicles mentioned above.

As for air transport, we will have control of existing airports. We can continue operating them—taking the related jobs and charging the related landing and terminal and gate fees. We will identify pilots among us and, if we think it judicious and economically sound, maybe the governments of our territories will jointly organize an airline to ply air routes that are critical to our existence and survival. It goes without saying that we will expand our airports and air transport services as demand increases.

Financial Services

This is a hard one. Black Americans are peculiar when it comes to money. We do not seem to mind White Americans knowing how much money we have in the bank. However, we seem to care a great deal about Black Americans knowing how much money we have in the bank. Unfortunately, we appear to do almost everything in our power to avoid Black banks. We will have to have a mind-reset on this issue. It will be important to have a strong financial system in the territories. That means having sufficient monetary liquidity in the system, which can be generated by placing our money in what will become Black owned/controlled and operated banks. This lack of Black money trust is a problem that we must overcome.

It is important to note that, at least initially, because we will be living and operating as US citizens, we will most likely be using US dollars to conduct transactions. This means that the banking system in the territories will be under the control of the Federal Reserve Bank, and depositors will benefit from protection under the Federal Deposit Insurance Corporation (FDIC). In the longer term, however, it is likely that we will be able to evolve some independence and establish our own currency. When that occurs, we may not be able to provide immediately FDIC-type coverage, therefore, we must count on our banks to be transparent and operate with great prudence. We recognize that this entire issue may be resolved if the banking system and currency that we evolve and allow to operate in the territories are of the digital currency variety.

In any event, financial services represent a critical need that must be met. Let us place our top economists and finance experts to work on sorting out how to manage this important system in the new territories.

Communications Services

As you know, fundamental communications services include telephone, television (cable), and the Internet. These systems will already be operational when we assume control of the territories. Given our new position in America as a result of the territorial grab, we must be cognizant of potential efforts to use these means of communication against us. Consequently, we should be careful concerning what transits our borders on a wired and wireless basis. We know that one of the biggest problems facing the so-called developing world is the false hopes and myths engendered by the western world vis-à-vis the people of the developing world via media. The shaping of thought (mind control) and the spreading of adverse stereotypical images of the Black people of the world is a core *modus operandi* of the Western media. Therefore, it is particularly important that we keep that which is useful and let the rest alone. We should assign the well-informed to monitor media in our territories to ensure that we are not affected adversely by the media. Favorably, given our demand for entertainment, we should create jobs and opportunities for creativity and growth by using media instruments to nurture and display the brilliant ideas of our people in the territories.

Wholesale/Retail Services

Here, the story is short. Black nationalism!!! We will have control of the territories. We will have Black American wholesalers and retailers operating in the territories. We should ensure that we have eliminated from our minds the "someone else's ice is colder" mentality and be prepared to support fully the Black business that arise. At the same time Black businesses should strive to conduct the highest-quality possible wholesale and retail services so that our people will have no reticence or qualms about patronizing Black businesses.

Conclusion

Black Americans have a great failing. We have imbibed the Christian faith so wholeheartedly that we believe that we can convert the most notorious sinner with the love of Christ. We forget that: (1) "Charity begins at home;" and (2) the task of destroying satan is left to the lamb (Christ himself). On the first count, we must turn inward and look after our own and provide for ourselves and for the generations to come. Territorial land grabs are a direct method for doing this. On the second count, let us leave satan to his own devices. Our actions as the lambs of God will upturn satan's kingdom. If you resist him, he will flee from you. Let us resist satanic America, which has practiced evil against us for over 400 years. Let us practice *Takeconomics* and take territories that are rightfully ours. We are American citizens and have every right to the land as any other American. If we choose to organize and migrate to a territory in large numbers sufficient to swamp the existing population, then we have every right to own and control the territory. We shall have the land, the banks, the businesses, the jobs, the schools, and everything else that goes with the territory. We shall take it all to meet our needs. This is the "great substance" that is to accompany the exodus that is written about in the literature.

We will take the territories and occupy existing cities and towns. And we will build new Black towns and cities like those that were developed by our forefathers following the Civil War in the West wherever they could find unoccupied territory—but on a much larger scale. In time, we will be able to see again our thriving Black Wall Streets and Harlems without the mayhem of "honkies" who came into our former spaces seeking the pleasure of our art, food, music, and women. We have proven over and over again that we are the people of God. It is written and must now come to pass that the Blessings of God are for the People of God.

When we take these territories and establish ourselves in the land it will invigorate and strengthen our faith. It will cause us to have and walk with a pride that we have never known in these lands. The cycle will complete itself and our wise men of millennia past will be proven true. It will be manifest for all men to see together that God is Great. SHe will have guided Heris people—once a nothing people—to create a nation for ourselves through our own action. At that time, we can stand back in awe and smile—even laugh joyously—knowing that our God has not failed us. SHe will have done what SHe always does: Make something Great out of absolutely nothing! Most importantly, we will see God as we should. Not as some distant heavenly figure who does not display our likeness. Rather we will see God in the faces of all of those around us (for we are all gods, children of the most-high God).

While there are those who argue that we should not follow this path and cordon ourselves off into separate territories because it minimizes the enemies effort to contain and strangle us, we respond that the "light is on." Just as the entire world came to know about George Floyd's murder and protested widely and vigorously, any attempt to impose undue harm on a Black state in the US would raise the ire of the entire world against the US. Given the US's increasingly dependent and declining position in the world economy it stands to reason that the nation would not risk drawing upon itself economic and other types of pressure and sanctions from the rest of the world by attacking a Black state in any harmful and indiscriminate way.

Today's technological world means that lies cannot stand. The truth comes to light ultimately. Therefore, Black America can use the protection provided by our technological world to effect territorial land grabs and to build essentially Black states knowing that the light is on for the world to see. At the same time, we can use the technology to keep in the world's vision the incalculable injustices that have been perpetrated against Black America for over 400 years. The related and accompanying logic is that history informs us and the rest of the world that one known solution to America's injustice is separation—Black from White. It is against this backdrop that we can exodus and initiate Black independent living in the not so good ole US of A.

Appendix A.—List of Fundamental Migration Variables and Their Interpretations.

No.	Migration Variables	Interpretation
1	White majority population size	The size of the White population over Black population; the smaller the better for a territorial grab.
2	Median age of population	The older the better; reduces the time period during which Whites will occupy the territory.
3	State GDP (billions of dollars)	The larger the better; a proxy for the level of development of the economy in a state.
4	Number of employed persons	The larger the better; indicates a state economy's capacity to accommodate workers.
5	Land area (square miles)	The larger the better; indicates a state's capacity to accommodate populations.
6	Arable land (crop land 1,000 acres)	The larger the better; indicates a state's capacity to produce food.
7	Water surface (square miles)	The larger the better; indicates a state's capacity to accommodate populations.
8	Annual precipitation 2019 (inches)	The more the better; indicates a state's capacity to accommodate populations.
9	Cooling degree days	The more the better; indicates the warmth of a state and, thereby, its capacity to produce agriculture and an absence of a need for heat energy.
10	Heating degree days	The fewer the better; indicates the coolness of a state and, thereby, its incapacity to produce agriculture and its need for heat energy.
11	Miles of public road	The more the better; indicates ease of access to a state's territory.

No.	Migration Variables	Interpretation
12	Miles of freight railroad	The more the better; indicates ease of access to a state's territory.
13	Bridges (number)	The fewer the better; bridges can be complex, and difficult and expensive to upkeep.
14	Forest use (1,000 acres)	The more the better; indicates the availability of timber for a variety of uses.
15	Hunting and Fishing (value of licenses; thousands of dollars)	The more the better; indicates a state's natural capacity to produce food.
16	Grass and pasture lands (1,000 acres)	The more the better; indicates a state's capacity to accommodate cattle and to produce related goods.
17	Major airports	The more the better; indicates ease of access to a state's territory.
18	Total local governments	The larger the better; indicates a state's level of development and its capacity to accommodate populations.
19	Existing housing units	The larger the better; indicates a state's capacity to provide housing for populations.
20	Energy production (trillions of BTUs)	The more the better; proxies for volume/value of energy reserves.
21	Mineral production (thousands of dollars)	The more the better; proxies for volume/value of mineral reserves.
22	Colleges and universities	The more the better; indicates a state's capacity to generate knowledge and produce trained professionals.
23	Number of hospitals	The more the better; indicates a state's capacity to manage a population's health.

No.	Migration Variables	Interpretation
24	Spending on public elementary and secondary education (dollars, millions)	The more the better; indicates a state's capacity to generate resources for educating the young.

Source: The author

Appendix B.—Sources: Migration Variables Statistics

No.	Migration Variables	Data Sources
1	White majority population size	U.S. Department of Commerce. Census Bureau. Annual Estimates of the Resident Population by Sex, Race, and Hispanic Origin, April 1, 2010 - July 1, 2019. https://www.census.gov/data/tables/time-series/demo/popest/2010s-state-detail.html; retrieved October 3, 2020. (White population less Black population)
2	Median age of population	U.S. Department of Commerce. Census Bureau. Annual Estimates of the Resident Population by Selected Age Groups by Sex, April 1, 2010 - July 1, 2019. https://www.census.gov/data/tables/time-series/demo/popest/2010s-state-detail.html; retrieved October 3, 2020.
3	State GDP (billions of dollars)	U.S. Department of Commerce. Bureau of Economic Analysis. Gross Domestic Product by State (2019). www.bea.gov; retrieved October 4, 2020.
4	Number of employed persons	U.S. Department of Labor. Bureau of Labor Statistics. State Employment and Unemployment. Table 4. Employees on nonfarm payrolls by state and selected industry sector, NSA (July 2019). https://www.bls.gov/news.release/laus.t04.htm; retrieved on October 4, 2020.
5	Land area (square miles)	U.S. Department of Commerce. Census Bureau. State Area Measurements and Internal Points Coordinates. https://www.census.gov/geographies/reference-files/2010/geo/state-area.html; retrieved on October 2, 2020.

No.	Migration Variables	Data Sources
6	Arable land (crop land 1,000 acres)	U.S. Department of Agriculture, Economic Research Service. https://www.ers.usda.gov/data-products/major-land-uses/maps-and-state-rankings-of-major-land-uses/; retrieved on October 2, 2020.
7	Water surface (square miles)	U.S. Department of Commerce. Census Bureau. State Area Measurements and Internal Points Coordinates. https://www.census.gov/geographies/reference-files/2010/geo/state-area.html; retrieved on October 2, 2020.
8	Annual precipitation 2019 (inches)	Statista.com. Annual Precipitation in the United States 2019, by State. https://www.statista.com/statistics/1101518/annual-precipitation-by-us-state/; retrieved on October 2, 2020.
9	Cooling degree days	U.S. Department of Energy. Energy Information Administration. Data for Wyoming and Montana are Mountain; North and South Dakota are West North Central. https://www.eia.gov/energyexplained/units-and-calculators/degree-days.php (deviations from 65 degrees (above) for 2019); retrieved on October 2, 2020.
10	Heating degree days	U. S. Department of Energy. Energy Information Administration. Data for Wyoming and Montana are Mountain; North and South Dakota are West North Central. https://www.eia.gov/energyexplained/units-and-calculators/degree-days.php (deviations from 65 degrees (below) for 2019); retrieved on October 2, 2020.
11	Miles of public road	U.S. Department of Transportation. Bureau of Transportation Statistics. States by the Numbers. https://www.bts.gov/content/state-transportation-numbers; retrieved on October 2, 2020.

No.	Migration Variables	Data Sources
12	Miles of freight railroad	U.S. Department of Transportation. Bureau of Transportation Statistics. States by the Numbers. https://www.bts.gov/content/state-transportation-numbers; retrieved on October 2, 2020.
13	Bridges (number)	U.S. Department of Transportation. Bureau of Transportation Statistics. States by the Numbers. https://www.bts.gov/content/state-transportation-numbers; retrieved on October 2, 2020.
14	Forest use (1,000 acres)	U.S. Department of Agriculture, Economic Research Service. https://www.ers.usda.gov/data-products/major-land-uses/maps-and-state-rankings-of-major-land-uses/; retrieved on October 2, 2020.
15	Hunting and Fishing (value of licenses; thousands of dollars)	U.S. Department of the Interior. Fish and Wildlife Service. Value (Gross Cost) of Hunting and Fishing Licenses/Permits Sold during 2019. https://www.fws.gov/wsfrprograms/Subpages/LicenseInfo/Natl%20Hunting%20License%20Report%202019.pdf and https://www.fws.gov/wsfrprograms/Subpages/LicenseInfo/Natl%20Fishing%20License%20Report%202019.pdf; retrieved October 6, 2020.
16	Grass and pasture lands (1,000 acres)	U.S. Department of Agriculture, Economic Research Service. https://www.ers.usda.gov/data-products/major-land-uses/maps-and-state-rankings-of-major-land-uses/; retrieved on October 2, 2020.
17	Major airports	U.S. Department of Transportation. Bureau of Transportation Statistics. States by the Numbers. https://www.bts.gov/content/state-transportation-numbers; retrieved on October 2, 2020.

No.	Migration Variables	Data Sources
18	Total local governments	U.S. Department of Commerce. Census Bureau. US 2017 Census of Government. Table 2.--Local Governments by Type and State. https://www.census.gov/data/tables/2017/econ/gus/2017-governments.html; retrieved on October 3, 2020.
19	Existing housing units	U.S. Department of Commerce. Census Bureau. National, State, and County Housing Units Total, 2010-2019. https://www.census.gov/data/datasets/time-series/demo/popest/2010s-total-housing-units.html; retrieved October 3, 2020.
20	Energy production (trillions of BTUs)	U.S. Department of Energy. Energy Information Administration. State Profiles and Energy Estimates. Natural Gas and Crude Oil Production for 2017. https://www.eia.gov/state/; retrieved on October 9, 2020.
21	Mineral production (thousands of dollars)	U.S. Geological Service. State Mineral Statistics and Information. Nonfuel Mineral Commodity Production for 2016. https://www.usgs.gov/centers/nmic/state-minerals-statistics-and-information; retrieved on October 9, 2020.
22	Colleges and universities	U.S. Department of Education. National Center for Education Statistics. Table 317.20. Degree-granting postsecondary institutions, by control and classification of institution and state or jurisdiction: 2015-16. https://nces.ed.gov/programs/digest/d16/tables/dt16_317.20.asp; retrieved October 3, 2020.

No.	Migration Variables	Data Sources
23	Number of hospitals	U.S. Department of Labor. Bureau of Labor Statistics. Number of Hospitals and Hospital Employment in Each State, Third Quarter of 2019. https://www.bls.gov/opub/ted/2020/number-of-hospitals-and-hospital-employment-in-each-state-in-2019.htm; retrieved October 4, 2020.
24	Spending on public elementary and secondary education (dollars, millions)	U.S. Department of Education. National Center for Education Statistics. Digest of Education Statistics. Table 326.25, Current Expenditure for Public Elementary and Secondary Education, by State or Selected Jurisdictions, 1969-70 - 2016/17. https://nces.ed.gov/programs/digest/d19/tables/dt19_236.25.asp; retrieved on October 4, 2020.

Source: The author

Appendix C.—Summary of Migration Statistics by State

No.	Migration Variables	Wyoming	South Dakota	North Dakota	Montana
1	White majority population size	527,904	727,738	636,571	943,822
2	Median age of population	38	37	35	40
3	State GDP (billions of dollars)	40	55	57	53
4	Number of employed persons (thousands)	297	445	439	492
5	Land area (square miles)	97,093	75,811	69,001	145,546
6	Arable land (crop land 1,000 acres)	1,986	19,355	27,121	16,605
7	Water surface (square miles)	720	1,305	1,698	1,494
8	Annual precipitation 2019 (inches)	18	31	24	21
9	Cooling degree days	1,397	954	954	1,397
10	Heating degree days	5,308	7,073	7,073	5,308
11	Miles of public road	29,666	82,501	88,050	73,573
12	Miles of freight railroad	1,890	2,029	3,287	3,719
13	Bridges (number)	3,129	5,824	4,355	5,265
14	Forests (timber land)	7,002	1,789	517	18,429

No.	Migration Variables	Wyoming	South Dakota	North Dakota	Montana
15	Hunting and Fishing (value of licenses; thousands of dollars)	32,453	29,325	15,762	34,678
16	Hunting	46,086	24,972	13,336	47,629
17	Major airports	9	5	8	9
18	Total local governments	794	1,996	2,664	1,226
19	Existing housing units	280,291	401,862	380,173	519,935
20	Energy production (trillions of BTUs)	2,222	8	3,093	169
21	Mineral production (thousands of dollars)	2,290,000	367,000	97,300	905,000
22	Colleges and universities	10	25	20	22
23	Number of hospitals	32	76	73	85
24	Spending on public elementary and secondary education (dollars, millions)	1,555	1,379	1,510	1,689

Source: The author

Appendix D.—State-Wise Ranking of Unweighted Migration Variables

No.	Migration Variables	Wyoming	South Dakota	North Dakota	Montana
1	White majority population size	1	3	2	4
2	Median age of population	2	3	4	1
3	State GDP (billions of dollars)	4	2	1	3
4	Number of employed persons (thousands)	4	2	3	1
5	Land area (square miles)	2	3	4	1
6	Arable land (crop land 1,000 acres)	4	2	1	3
7	Water surface (square miles)	4	3	1	2
8	Annual precipitation 2019 (inches)	1	2	2	3
9	Cooling degree days	1	2	2	1
10	Heating degree days	1	2	2	1
11	Miles of public road	4	2	1	3
12	Miles of freight railroad	4	3	2	1
13	Bridges (number)	1	4	2	3
14	Forest use (1,000 acres)	2	3	4	1

EXODUS

No.	Migration Variables	Wyoming	South Dakota	North Dakota	Montana
15	Hunting and Fishing (value of licenses; thousands of dollars)	2	3	4	1
16	Grass and pasture lands (1,000 acres)	2	3	4	1
17	Major airports	1	3	2	1
18	Total local governments	4	2	1	3
19	Existing housing units	4	2	3	1
20	Energy production (trillions of BTUs)	2	4	1	3
21	Mineral production (thousands of dollars)	1	3	4	2
22	Colleges and universities	4	1	3	2
23	Number of hospitals	4	2	3	1
24	Spending on public elementary and secondary education (dollars, millions)	2	4	3	1

Source: The author

Chapter Six: Point Zero Nation Formation Revisited

Introduction

This chapter is derived from, and reflects modifications to, Essay Three of *Chosen: Black America's Calling*.[53] It tells the story of a second pathway through which Black Americans can experience independent living in the wilderness of North America. As opposed to positing that Black America engage in territorial land grabs to capture and transform selected states as outlined in Chapter Five, here we elaborate on a different scenario. In this new scenario, we posit that the broader nation goes through a soul searching process, determines that it is only good and right that Black Americans be extended some of what we helped them get, and awards to us valuable lands that we can use for our own independent living in a "nation formation" context.

The chapter begins by painting a backdrop to how reparatory justice might be realized for Black Americans. We add to the canvass an analysis of how the nation can be constituted initially from an administrative perspective. We finalize the picture by using our expertise to apply broad brush strokes that provide perspectives on how the nation's socioeconomic framework should be fashioned. Finally, we emphasize that a phased approach should be adopted for creating a homeland for Black Americans. A judicious warning is in order here as this chapter does not provide complete and thorough starting-point-to-ending-point guidance on how a new Black American nation (Shabazzland/Zion) can be realized. Rather, it serves as a portrait that can help Black Americans who engage in exodus imagine a process that can take us to future nation formation. Those Black Americans

---

[53] See Brooks Robinson. (2010) *Chosen: Black America's Calling*. BlackEconomics.org: Honolulu.

must perform the arduous, yet surprisingly straightforward, task of bringing the nation into being with all of its potential perfections and imperfections.

Reparatory Justice

House Resolution 40 and Senate Bill 1038, while somewhat inadequate, provide an opportunity for the United States Congress and Government to begin a soul searching process and acknowledging the historical wrongs that have been imposed on Black Americans for over 400 years.[54] Let us assume for sake of argument that this legislation passes the US Congress and a President signs it. Such passing could—in today's world of ZOOM, WEBEX, YouTube, and other technologies—facilitate a broad and wide-ranging national discussion concerning how Black Americans should be repaired for historical and incalculable injustices.

Given expected US financial conditions in the period ahead, we have argued that Black Americans should not accept reparations mainly in the form of cash. Why? Because the value of dollars is likely to decline going forward for at least two reasons. First, borrowing and spending in response to the current Covid-19 Pandemic and to stimulate a US economic recovery will render US Government debt unsustainable, which will reduce the value of the dollar. Second, if Black Americans accept reparations mainly in the form of cash, then there will be a large infusion of cash into the US economy. Without a significant increase in production, this cash infusion will be inflationary and will also decrease the value of the dollar.

---

[54] For an analysis of the bills' shortcomings see Brooks Robinson. (2019) "HR 40 and SB 1038: More Time, Money, and Direction." https://www.blackeconomics.org/BELit/mtmd.pdf; retrieved October 17, 2020.

In a high inflation US economy, Black Americans' acquisition of financial and nonfinancial assets using reparations payments will not produce wealth equalizing outcomes—Black versus White. Rather, Whites will receive payments for their highly inflated financial and nonfinancial assets, then invest those funds in higher quality assets in more favorable, less inflationary environments. When efforts are undertaken to wring inflation out of the US economy, then the prices of assets obtained by Blacks will collapse. At that stage, Black Americans will have more assets than before reparations, but the value of those assets will be depressed, while Whites will have been able to preserve their wealth advantage. Therefore, receiving reparations payments mainly in the form of cash would be a mistake.

Besides, if independent living is the ultimate aim of Black Americans, then the acquisition of assets in the US would be an illogical development. Consequently, we have advocated that Black Americans seek reparations from the US Government in an amenable environment in the following three forms: (1) Land; (2) resources/materiel; and (3) international support.[55]

In an amenable environment in which the US Government is willing to repair Black Americans in a favorable form we should take federally owned lands to meet the bill. As was the case in Chapter Five where we analyzed conditions and resources in states to determine the states that were most favorable for territorial land grabs, similar types of analyses should be performed by Black Americans to determine the

---

[55] See Brooks Robinson. (2015) "A Broad Three-Point Reparations Program for US Afrodescendants Versus
CARICOM's 10-Point Program." Black Economics.org. (March) https://www.blackeconomics.org/BELit/btprp.pdf; retrieved October 17, 2020.

federally-owned lands that should be accepted as partial fulfillment of US Government reparations requirements.[56]

In addition to federally owned lands, the US Government should be prepared to provide resources and materiel that can be used to build physical and human infrastructure (capital) for Shabazzland/Zion. Also, the US Government should be willing to assist the new nation in landing memberships in key international organizations that open the door to Black Americans realizing full nationhood and taking our rightful place as a participant in decision-making for Earth along with other nations. We will discuss these latter two reparations requirements later in this chapter.

Administrative Aspects of Nation Formation

With a pledge of land, resources/materiel, and international support in hand, Black Americans can begin development of Shabazzland/Zion administratively. Loosely, this entails forming a governance and political structure, and using that structure to envision a socioeconomic structure and a phased process for actualization of the nation. This is all depicted in Figure 1 (next page).

Given the broader nation's approval of nation formation by Black Americans, efforts to organize Shabazzland/Zion administratively should be straightforward—albeit elongated. The first requirement is to assemble an initial decisions body (committee, team, or task force) to initiate the process that is outlined in this chapter. Logically, certain members of the initial decisions body would derive from those selected to perform the research called for in HR 40 and SB 1038. Those with knowledge concerning how Black

---

[56] Op. cit. (2010). *Chosen: Black America's Calling.* pp.75 and 108-112.

Figure 1.–Pathway to Shabazzland's/Zion's Development

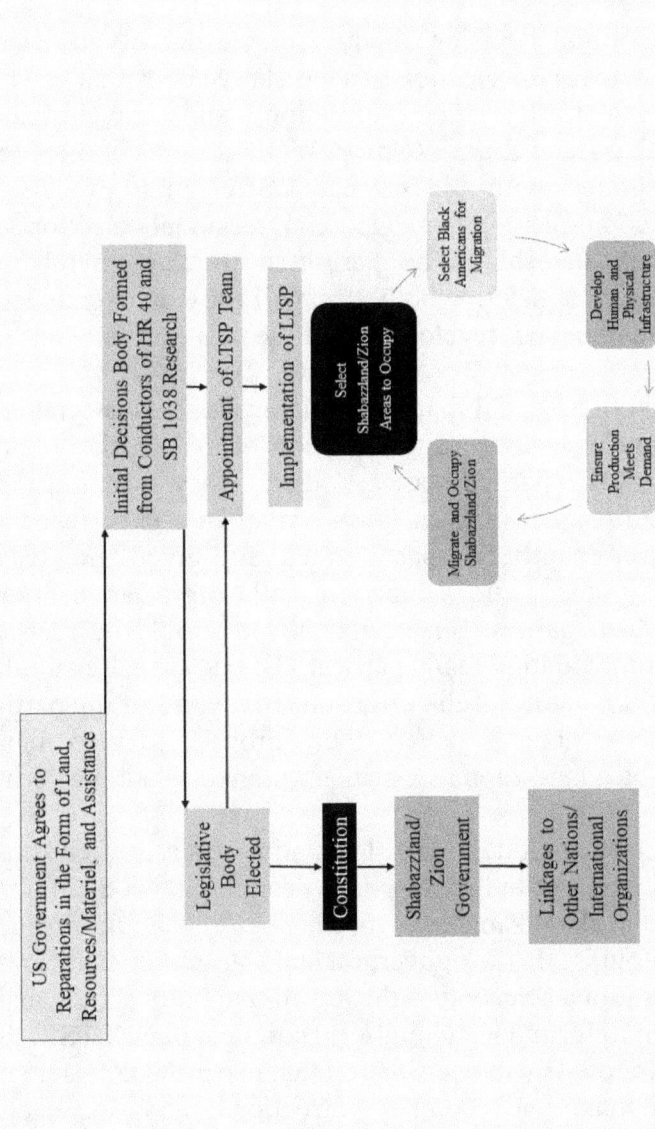

Source: The author

Americans evolved historically should have important insights concerning how Black Americans can best organize an independent living arrangement.

The initial decisions body's first order of business is to arrange for the election of a legislative body that can provide oversight for the formation and development of Shabazzland/Zion. We propose that this election process be integrated with the normal US election process. As a subcomponent of a US congressional election, Black Americans should be permitted to elect members of a separate legislative body that will provide oversight for the formation and development of the new nation.

It is not essential that political parties surface symbiotically during the runup to the election of the legislative body. If political parties arise, then they should remain unconstrained. Given Black America's experience with a predominantly two-party system and given knowledge that many other nations function well with a larger volume of political parties, Shabazzland/Zion should be receptive to accommodating many parties. The one caveat to all of this is that, by nature of the effort underway, all of the parties that arise should have the proper development of Shabazzland/Zion as a primary plank in their platforms.

Once constituted, the legislative body's first order of business should be to design a constitution for Shabazzland/Zion, which, *inter alia*, should include the contours of the governmental structure that is to be operational. Secondly, the legislative body should appoint a team to formulate a long-term strategic plan (LTSP) that can be adopted by the new nation that has provisions for periodic revisions and course corrections. As expected, the constitution should circumscribe the scope of permissible actions in the new nation, and the LTSP should provide a roadmap for development. Together (the constitution and LTSP) should serve as the foundation on which Shabazzland/Zion is constructed.

It is important to keep in mind that all Black Americans may not migrate to Shabazzland/Zion to enjoy Black independent living. Nevertheless, there are likely to be tens of millions who opt to live in the new homeland. Such a large population cannot simply up and relocate. Accordingly, we anticipate a phased approach to settlement.

The following phased evolution of Shabazzland/Zion should be reflected in the aforementioned LTSP: (i) Occupation of already developed locations in the homeland; (ii) a first round of infrastructure development for selected undeveloped areas of the homeland; (iii) occupation of areas completed during the first round of infrastructure development; and (iv) subsequent rounds of infrastructure development and occupation. Consistent with this phased approach for development, the LTSP should synchronize in-time training of Black Americans so that we are prepared to fulfill our duties and responsibilities when we are approved by the Shabazzland/Zion Government to migrate to the homeland. This phased training will occur while Black Americans reside in the US and will draw upon the resources that are pledged to fulfill reparations requirement. That is, the LTSP must anticipate the entire breadth and scope of early socioeconomic developments in the new nation by not only accounting for the development itself, but also for all factors that will facilitate and ensure successful implementation of the development process.

Shabazzland's/Zion's Socioeconomic Framework

The arising of Shabazzland/Zion means that an entire society will form in new surroundings and under unique circumstances. Black Americans, who will inhabit the land, will bring an entire culture and set of life experiences, processes, and behaviors. However, the extent to which the transplanting will not preserve identically existing arrangements in the US, we are likely to find that certain aspects of our socioeconomic experience will be transformed. Here, we intend to touch on only socioeconomic factors and ignore the many other aspects of life: Religion, psychology, culture, history, etc. By "socioeconomic," we mean those factors that contribute directly to our ability to produce material goods and services that ensure our well-being. Specifically, we encompass in the term "socioeconomic" education, health, employment, income, business, finance, and other economic factors that will determine our material living standard. We recommend the adoption of certain perspectives with respect to these socioeconomic factors.

But before offering these perspectives, we issue a round of sound advice to those developing Shabazzland's/Zion's LTSP: "Use existing technology." That is, use access to the world's pantheon of experiences for all of these socioeconomic factors to learn and analyze best practices before coming away with recommendations for the nation. Also, while engaged in the just-mentioned exercise do not fail to consider old and new standards and methods. While new standards and methods may imply "cutting-edge," what we know from "Climate Change," is that the adoption of "new and improved," can often translate into disastrous results in time.

Education.—The overarching objective should be to ensure that every citizen of Shabazzland/Zion attains the highest level of education required and desired to achieve life goals. Because life goals change, opportunities should always be available for learning to occur. There should be no hesitancy in adopting new educational modalities that are not harmful and that have been proven to be effective and, at the same time, in dispensing with educational modalities that are absent these characteristics. To the extent possible, the cost of learning (education) should be borne by the state.

Health.—The nation should look upon healthcare as a human right. However, Shabazzland/Zion should adopt a practice of continuous teaching and advocacy for healthy lifestyles; i.e., consuming appropriate and high-quality foods, engaging in regular exercise, and avoiding substance abuse (prescription and nonprescription). The adage that "an ounce of prevention is worth a pound of cure" should be healthcare providers' vaunted position. To the extent possible, the cost of healthcare should be borne by the state.

Employment.—Our world of tomorrow may entail little-to-no human labor. While human labor remains, those citizens who prefer to perform labor should be guaranteed a job by the state. Those citizens who do not prefer to perform traditional labor should be monitored for their performance of non-traditional-labor to ensure that they produce something of value for the nation—even if that production is limited to happiness that is compensated for with "hapines."[57] For Shabazzland/Zion emphasis should be placed on permitting engagement in activities (work) of highest value for the citizen. In addition, it seems reasonable that the state should attempt to invert today's typical work-life scenario by permitting potential workers to enjoy expanded non-work liberties during their youth, but to offset those early freedoms with more opportunities to work later in life.

Income.—The production of essential goods and services should be valued equally in Shabazzland/Zion. Compensation for that production should be as uniform as possible, which should help constrain deviations from income and wealth equality.

Business.—The adage, "if it exists, then it must be efficient, otherwise it wouldn't exist," appears to have relevance in today's world and, potentially, in the world of tomorrow. In this context, it appears that the persistent reoccurrence of highly concentrated industries versus competitive industries signals that large firms that operate as monopolists, duopolists, or oligopolists have efficacy. If this is true, then we can expect for monopolies, duopolies, and oligopolies to dominate business production ultimately in Shabazzland/Zion. Given this

---

[57] "Hapines" are discussed by Brooks Robinson. (2015) "The Economics of Freedom for Black Americans in a Technological World: A Brief Futuristic Essay." BlackEconomics.org. https://www.blackeconomics.org/BEFuture/tefba.pdf; retrieved on October 17, 2020.

outcome, it may be prudent to adopt favorable aspects of a China-type state capitalism business model. However, this model should be modified to include a 100 percent estate tax. That is, entrepreneurs who build mega business empires will be unable to pass all of their wealth on to their descendants—it should inure to the state.

Finance.—Shabazzland's/Zion's financial structure is highly likely to operate using digital currencies. At that time, there are likely to be new and efficient financial instruments that perform the three functions that money serves today.[58] Also, at that time, new tools would have surfaced for managing liquidity in the economy, controlling inflation, and ensuring optimal growth—*inter alia*. We offer dual guidance for those who will manage Shabazzland's/Zion's financial sector. First, make every effort to design and implement a financial system for the nation that is not based on debt (i.e., adopt a system that is a variation on an improved form of Islamic financing). Second, those who manage the financial sector should not have intervention as a first policy response. With respect to the latter guidance, it will likely be shown by the time we reach Shabazzland/Zion that economies whose monetary authorities were less interventionist experienced the best economic outcomes in

---

[58] The three functions of money are to serve as: (i) a unit of account; (ii) a medium of exchange; and (iii) a store of value.

the long run. Also, this second guidance is buttressed by the realization that Shabazzland's/Zion's government and financial system should focus predominantly on ensuring the well-being of citizens, not the well-being of business institutions—to the extent that these two can be addressed separately.

Economy.—We have long advocated a type of regionalization of the world according to production with comparative advantage accompanied by trade to meet remaining demand. The economists who will help formulate Shabazzland's/Zion's LTSP must identify those goods and services for which the nation will have comparative advantage and organize the economy around that production. Admittedly, it is also wise to be as self-sufficient as possible in the production of strategic goods and services. It is not rocket science to strike a balance between these two production decisions. As already noted, all of this should be managed in a "state capitalism" environment with a 100 percent estate tax. This latter arrangement, while excellent for the long-term benefit of the nation and income and wealth equality, could present challenges for motivating favorable incentives for entrepreneurship and innovation. We can only suggest that the state find other tools to generate entrepreneurial and innovative behaviors.

These recommended perspectives or positions on socioeconomic factors are, in many ways, contrary to today's *status quo*. Nevertheless, we advise those who are to formulate Shabazzland's/Zion's LTSP to assess them carefully before rejecting them. Also, our perspectives will present certain challenges for achievement. This is all the more reason why the legislative body that will select advisers to produce the LTSP must choose those who are most skilled to perform the task. Shabazzland/Zion presents a new opportunity to do things differently—better. Who more than Black Americans deserve a nation whose socioeconomic environment and outcomes shine brightly and high in comparison with the rest of the world's nations? As the old saying goes: "If there is a will, then there is a way."

Phased Actualization of Shabazzland/Zion

During 1947 Partition in India when Muslims headed to East and West Pakistan territories and Hindus departed those territories for India, millions went on the march to achieve nation formation in one fell swoop. This movement produced numerous logistical nightmares and created many socioeconomic problems that have not been resolved to this day. Nearly 75 years later we are discussing here the potential movement of millions of Black Americans to Shabazzland/Zion. We are wiser now and we can operationalize the migration better.

As Figure 1 highlights, the key to successful Black American nation formation is a phased approach to occupation of Shabazzland/Zion. Some areas in the new nation will be developed and can be occupied immediately. However, much of the new territory is likely to be undeveloped. Accordingly, the legislative body and the team that formulates the LTSP must gather a tremendous amount of data concerning the expertise inherent in the Black American population, and then to match that expertise with the needs and expected demands of the nation. Besides full knowledge of the resources available in the land to be occupied, successful formulation of a LTSP will entail knowing, *inter alia*: (i) Who will constitute the nation's population; (ii) which goods and services can that population produce; (iii) which goods and services must be produced to meet the population's demands; (iv) what will be produced versus what will be imported; (v) what will be exported; and (vi) from whence will the resources be derived to purchase the imports. The analysis is made more complex because the size and capacities of the population will continue to change over time. For experts with various digital databases and models, this is all a doable task. Now let us assume that a "perfect" LTSP can be formulated. How can successful implementation be assured?

The answer boils down to effective governance and resources. The legislative body that is elected must have full support and allegiance from the Black American population. In addition, the US Government must be fully committed to providing the financial and other resources and materiel that it has committed to meet the reparations bill, which will be required by the legislative body and the broader Shabazzland/Zion Government to operationalize the LTSP. Further assurance of successful implementation of the LTSP may also come from other nations who may support this Black American nation formation effort. If there is a favorable confluence of these events, then the nation formation process can unfold smoothly.

Another cautionary note is in order before concluding this chapter. The expert team that formulates and assists in implementing the LTSP must be cognizant of, and vigilant about, the need to calibrate the phased occupation of Shabazzland/Zion so that there is a nearly perfect balance of production and consumption by the resident population. This means that migration of the Black American population to Shabazzland/Zion must be regulated to perfection. This, in turn, means that Black Americans who have not yet migrated to Shabazzland/Zion are fully informed about, and agree to, their duties and responsibilities in the new nation in advance of their arrival, and that they engage proactively to ensure that they possess the knowledge, skills, and abilities required when they arrive in Shabazzland/Zion. In addition, this means that educational, training, and other institutions in the US and elsewhere remain committed to providing required services that were pledged to fulfill the reparations bill. The upshot of all of this is that, when the phased occupation of Shabazzland/Zion is managed properly, we will avoid shortages and/or wastage—two outcomes that are antithetical to a smoothly operating and efficient economy.

Conclusion

You may be a disbeliever that reparatory justice will ever come and/or you may be a naysayer on a decision by Black America to opt for independent living—either through territorial land grabs or through an amenable nation formation effort. If you are, then we invite you to consider the Black American and the world's response to George Floyd's murder and the murder of so many other Black Americans during the recent past. The level of social action in response to these events was somewhat surprising and more vigorous and enduring than expected. Importantly, the social action resulted in a wide range of marginal changes.

It is understood that changes are designed to pacify. However, we should see that certain changes that occurred serve as fuel for a next round of social actions in response to new and different social injustices against Black America. You need not doubt that new social injustices will occur. American history has been, and will continue to be, rooted in identifying new and bleak oppressive actions against Black Americans. American anti-Black racism is organic and systemic. What we can expect is an acceleration and intensification of social actions against this oppression.

The fact that American anti-Black racism is perpetual, and that the American system is unable to strike an undo key, means that social justice pressure will rise to the point of exploding and producing territorial land grabs and/or passage of HR 40 and SB 1038, which should lead to a reparations settlement. If Black Americans are wise, then nation formation will ensue. And if nation formation is approached systematically and in phases, then Black Americans can create an excellent Shabazzland/Zion for independent living—a haven in the wilderness of North America. This will represent a realization of the exodus about which we speak.

Chapter Seven: Exodus or Else

As a highly religious group some Black Americans defer to Dr. Martin Luther King's often recited sentiment that the "moral arc of the universe may be long, but it bends toward justice." The latter sentiment demands patience and could be interpreted to imply enduring with inaction. Other Black Americans have, without doubt, adopted a much more activist stance. This book embraces the latter position and advocates overt efforts to extricate Black Americans from an abusive American relationship. For those who say, "God will work it out," we say, "yes, SHe will work it out through our purposeful action." Why should we risk realizing that the bending of the moral arc is so long as to be ineffectual? Rather, with self-justification we must realize that we have the wherewithal to bend the moral arc on our own behalf to produce a favorable outcome. As casual observation of ongoing developments and what follows below make clear, Black America's failure to act is a shoehorn into a vanishing act.

Simply put, if Black America's lack of knowledge or weakness result in a failure to bring into existence an exodus in a form discussed in this book or otherwise, then we will ultimately be counted out on the world's future stage. Why? Because the enemy is at work to ensure our disappearance. We will disappear over time due to: (i) Amalgamation through interracial marriages; (ii) prison terms that prevent us from multiplying; (iii) purposeful discrimination against Black males that creates inequality between Black males and females who decide to not be unequally yoked and, thereby, fail to marry and produce offspring; (iv) lifestyle choices that create same-sex couples that produce no offspring; (v) poor health conditions for Black females who conceive and experience prenatal deaths or premature births that end in death; (vi) abortions; (vii) police murders; (viii) murder at the hands of Blacks or others; (ix) suicides; (x) deaths from increasingly prevalent natural disasters; (xi) viruses; and (xii) deaths by other unnatural causes. We can see the impact of all of these causes when we consider Black American population growth. For example, we can observe a general deceleration in Black America's population growth in the seven decades since 1950. For the 1950s, the Black population increased at an average annual rate of 2.21 percent; for the 1960s it grew 1.82 percent; for the 1970s, it grew 1.63 percent; for the 1980s it grew 1.28 percent; for the 1990s it grew 1.41 percent (a slight acceleration); for the first decade of the millennium it grew 1.17 percent; and for the second decade of the 21st century, it grew just 1.14 percent.[59] An extrapolation of such decelerating population growth into the future implies that Black America will soon experience a declining population.

To the extent that Black Americans survive, we have shown that neither Black nor White Americans can expect to live peaceably in this country. The "All it Takes is One" chapter shows that the power of history is sufficient to transform peace, no matter how long-lasting, into violence. The Donald J. Trump Presidency exacerbated the chasm between Blacks and other ethnic groups in America. Not only did hate crimes rise, but the general level of animus between groups rose. It does not matter that one can argue that the powerful elite orchestrated the driving of a wedge between groups in order to operationalize an age-old divide and conquer scheme. The fact of the matter is that Black and White

---

[59] These estimates are from the U.S. Census Bureau. (2012) Decennial Census of Population, 1940 to 2010, p. 9.
https://www.census.gov/newsroom/cspan/1940census/CSPAN_1940slides.pdf; retrieved on October 25, 2020. The 2020 estimate is based on the author's judgmental extrapolation of the 2019 Census Bureau population estimate to 2020, and the U.S. Census Bureau estimate of the 2019 Black American share of the population.

Americans continue to add to a history of dissimulation, which will serve as future grounds for violence. The 2020 Presidential election was indicative of the nation's divide on race, and a Biden presidency will not be sufficient to "heal the soul of America." It is the perpetual prospect for idiosyncratic or persistent violence in America that should cause Black Americans to conclude that an exodus is a must.

What should be convincing is that Black America does not have to invent the wheel. Exoduses have been achieved in the past. Chapter Four clarifies that, at bottom, nation formation (with or without migration) mainly requires a made-up mind. Granted, outcomes have not been perfect for certain newly formed nations. However, if one digs beneath the surface one will find that the nation formation efforts that we have discussed would have and could have proceeded much more smoothly had outside intervention been avoided. One must recognize that control of resources was a motivating factor in some nation formation efforts, and it was control of those resources that fueled confusion in nations after they formed. Accordingly, Black America must ensure that we prevent unwanted outside intervention after our new nation is formed.

A point that has not be highlighted sufficiently thus far is our individual planning today for tomorrow. Objective consideration would yield a clear picture on our preparedness for exodus. There is no question that Black Americans fill nearly every occupation in America today; however, our footprint in many important occupations is small. If we are to move on exodus in the near term—and this book suggests that we should—then we need to begin to urge our youth to scan the nation formation landscape and identify occupational gaps where more Black Americans will be required. Favorably, over the past seven decades, Black Americans have expanded our human capital tremendously by meeting higher educational requirements. Yet, today, we find ourselves to be degree rich, but skill poor. The literature is replete with examples of how the nation went from reflecting mainly Black American artisans and skilled mechanics and technicians in the past to reflecting very few Black Americans in many these types of occupations today. It is obvious that, as a nation, we will need those skilled at doing everything. Therefore, we must begin now to prepare for that eventual future need.

We are reminded daily to boil down issues/concerns to their essential nature. The late Professor John Henrick Clarke explained that "running a nation is like running a candy store."[60] As children all over America, we recall going into a local candy store and absorbing the simplicity of things and the joy of coming away with our favorite candy. If you perceived the operation of that candy store as simple, then you are prepared for nation formation. It is as simple as meeting needs, but with a higher level of complexity. But even the most complex of ideas can be explained simply. And no matter how complex, operating any system that is already in progress mainly boils down to making decisions about what to do when the system experiences a hiccup. What we find by observing American history and, indeed, the history of the Western World, is that operational decisions have often been made "on the fly." Decisionmakers have reached for and implemented the most obvious fixes. However, in the medium-to-long-term, many of the adopted solutions have proven to be faulty. Anybody can make it up as they go along. A truly great people use scientific knowledge and the wisdom of the elders to make decisions so that, for example, 100 years hence you do not find that fossil fuels and the greenhouse gases that they

---

[60] See Dr. John Henrick Clarke. (circa 1990s) "The Afrikan Mind, Part 1." https://www.youtube.com/watch?v=6TTWkr1OYp0; retrieved on November 8, 2020.

produce have destroyed the planet when renewable energies were available all along. In other words, Black Americans can do just as well or better on our own. We, too, know how to make it up as we go along. Hopefully, however, we will do it more wisely.

So, we are about to step on to the road to exodus. Whether we achieve exodus through territorial land grabs or through outright nation formation, we know in our heart of hearts that it is the correct thing to do. We must conclude that we are not so much in love with our former masters to be unable to loose him and let him go.

We must recognize that the world is on the verge of change. A change that will see the USA give way to Asia as the new center of the world economically and otherwise. The West has made its "contributions" to the evolution of the planet. However, because the elevation of Western Civilization was, and is, rooted in a lie (namely White Supremacy), the European's place in the world could not and cannot be very long-lasting.

Now add insult to injury. As America falls, Black Americans will increasingly be viewed as a burden. Many have argued that Black America has not been a burden for America in the past because of all of our economic, cultural, and scientific contributions. Purposely ignoring our role as producers, we recognize that Black America constitutes the margin of profitability for many American industries today. And, till now, "it's the economy stupid" has been the mantra. However, looking forward into an increasingly technological world where work as we know it is likely to disappear or be minimized considerably, and where the emphasis will be on conservation to save the planet, the task of supporting the consumption of non-White surplus labor is likely to be viewed unfavorably by White America. In this scenario, Black America's best bet is to escape and justify our existence as a separate nation.

In this book, we have provided who, what, when, where, why, and how answers to exodus. Now it is time for individual deep introspection with a goal of deciding to move forward with exodus. We know that "where the mind goes, the body follows." Collectively, we need to realize that, in fact, "we can do this." However, as one final pep talk and motivation for moving forward on independent living and/or nation formation, the following may suffice.

Let us never forget that the Black American nation constitutes one of the greatest nations in the history of the world. Why? We have been at war with White America, overtly or covertly, for over 400 years. We have lost many lives to the enemy. At the same time, we have taken many lives: Many of the unsolved murders of White Americans may reflect the silent and unacknowledged acts of Black men and women of taking justice into our own hands on dark roads, streets, and rooms all over this nation. Yet, through it all, we have survived and flourished in our own way. We have swollen in numbers from a score in 1619 to nearly 45 million in 2020. Tell us: Which nation has engaged one of, and the, most powerful nations in the world in war for 400 years and is still standing? Only Black America can make this claim. You can engage in semantics and call it something else, but by any objective measure, it has been war. We have won the war and live to tell the tale. All we have to do now is exodus, initiate independent living or nation formation so that we have the security required to continue living and growing in peace and to preserve our history and culture so that the world of today and tomorrow will know who these great Black American people are.

It is not that difficult a decision nor that difficult a strategy to finalize and operationalize. As we have already said: We just need a made-up mind. Once we make up our minds and decide not to look back, then we can take that first and momentous step on the road to exodus.

Index

Aaron, 26, 54
Abraham, 24
Addis Abbaba Accord, 39
Afghanistan, 18, 46
African, 5, 45, 69
Agriculture, 65, 80, 81
Allen
　Will, 65
Amalgamation, 104
Americas, 2, 45, 47
Amtrak, 69
Anderson
　Claud, 8
Ansari
　Sarah, 49
aquaponic, 65
Arabs, 39
Asaratnam
　Sinnappah, 35
assets, 55, 89
Bandaranaike
　S.W.R.D., 36
Belgians, 29
Belgium, 30
Bhutan, 10
Black America, ii, 2, 3, 4, 7, 8, 9, 10, 11, 12, 13, 14, 15, 16, 17, 18, 19, 20, 21, 22, 44, 49, 51, 52, 56, 62, 74, 88, 91, 93, 102, 104, 106, 108, 109
Black American, 1, 2, 4, 12, 14, 16, 17, 19, 21, 22, 44, 49, 59, 60, 66, 68, 72, 88, 100, 101, 102, 105, 107, 109
Black businesses, 72

Black nationalism, 64, 67, 72
Black Wall Streets, 73
Blacks, 2, 8, 11, 14, 15, 16, 17, 18, 19, 39, 51, 60, 61, 105
BLM, 11, 15
Bosnia, 26, 31, 32, 41
British, 28, 35, 39, 45, 49, 50
Brown
　H. Rap, 24, 67
Buckley-Zistel
　Susanne, 30
Buddha
　Gautama, 24
Buddhist, 24, 36
Business, 97
Canada, 48, 57
capitalism, 9, 98, 99
Caribbean, 56
Carmichael
　Stokely, 24
Catholics, 41
Cease Fire Agreement, 37
census, 55, 79, 80, 82, 105
Ceylon, 35
China, 17, 41, 46, 98
Christ, 73
Christian, 24, 73
Civil Rights, iii, 11
Civil War, 11, 16, 37, 73
Clarke
　John Henrick, 107
climate change, 57
Cold War, 32

Columbus
   Christopher, 45
Communications, 71
conditioned, 6, 9, 10, 14, 15
conditioning, 7, 9, 15
conflict, 12, 22, 23, 25, 26,
   27, 30, 33, 34, 35, 41, 42,
   43, 47
consumerism, 10
corruption, 64
coupe d'état, 30
Covid-19 pandemic, 89
Croatia, 32, 33
Croatians, 31
Croats, 32, 33, 34
Dalits, 27
Darfur, 39
Darity
   William, 8
death, 6, 37, 104
Delaware, 59, 62
discrimination, 104
Dorner
   Christopher Jordan, 19
Doshi
   Vidhi, 50, 51
drug addiction, 10
duopolists, 97
Eastern Orthodox
   Christians, 32
Economy, 64, 99
Education, 68, 82, 83, 95
Educational Services, 68
Egypt, 25, 26
Egyptians, 25, 26, 27, 41
Electric and Water Utilities,
   66
emigrants, 2, 52
emigrate, 47, 52

Employment, 79, 83, 96
entrepreneurs, 10, 98
equilibrium, 1, 22
escape, 8, 13, 14, 22, 23, 25,
   27, 29, 30, 31, 38, 58,
   109
Ethiopia, 41
ethnic cleansing, 33, 36
ethnic nationalism, 32, 33
Eurocentric, 17
Europe, 31, 45
exodus, ii, 1, 2, 3, 4, 5, 18,
   22, 23, 26, 44, 51, 52, 73,
   75, 88, 104, 106, 108,
   109, 110
FDIC, 71
Federal Deposit Insurance
   Corporation, 71
Field Negro, 20
Finance, 98
Financial Services, 70
Floyd
   George, iii, 74, 102
freedom, 2, 5, 6, 7, 13, 15,
   17, 18, 19, 20, 21, 45, 51,
   52, 70
Freedom, 6, 7, 17, 97
French, 45
Gandhi
   Mahatma, 25
Garang
   John, 40
geekism, 10
geniuses, 9
genocide, 29, 30, 31, 41
German-Jewish Holocaust,
   41
Germans, 29
global warming, 57

globalization, 11
gluttony, 10
Great Lakes, 57
Greyhound, 69
Gunaratna
    Rohan, 36
Habyarimana
    Juvénal, 30
Hamilton
    Darrick, 8
happiness, 10, 19, 96
Hari Kari, 12
Harlems, 73
Harris
    Kamala, 56
HBCUs, 15
Health, 68, 96
Health Services, 68
Hebrews, v, 4, 25, 26, 27, 41
Herzegovina, 26, 31, 41
Hindus, 26, 27, 28, 36, 41, 49, 50, 51, 100
history, iv, 2, 5, 9, 11, 12, 15, 22, 24, 25, 28, 29, 31, 41, 42, 44, 45, 46, 49, 51, 52, 67, 75, 95, 102, 105, 107, 109
Hitler
    Adolf, 24
Holbrooke
    Richard, 34
homeland, 21, 31, 44, 56, 88, 94
House Negro, 20
House Resolution 40, 89
Housing, 59, 66, 82
Howard University, 15
Hutus, 26, 29, 30, 31, 41

immigrants, 2, 44, 45, 48, 52
immigration, 2, 44, 49, 52
Imtiyaz
    A.R.M., 35
Income, 97
independence, 2, 6, 7, 13, 14, 15, 16, 17, 19, 20, 21, 29, 33, 35, 36, 39, 45, 49, 50, 51, 52, 71
India, 2, 26, 27, 28, 37, 41, 44, 46, 49, 50, 51, 100
inflation, 90, 98
injustice, 75
interracial marriages, 104
Iqbal
    Allama, 28, 29
Iraq, 18
Islamic, 24, 27, 31, 98
Israel, 4, 26, 27
Jaffna, 37
Jesus, 24
Jim Crow, iii, 11
JNA, 33
Joseph
    Brad, 32
Judeo-Christian, 24
justice, 19, 20, 24, 25, 27, 29, 30, 35, 38, 41, 54, 61, 88, 102, 103, 104, 109
Kagame
    Paul, 30, 31
Kayibanda
    Grégoire, 30
King
    Martin Luther, 25, 104
Kosovo, 32, 47
land, 3, 4, 13, 18, 19, 25, 52, 54, 56, 61, 73, 74, 76,

80, 81, 84, 86, 88, 90, 91, 95, 101, 102, 103, 108
leadership, 12, 13, 14, 15, 30, 33, 36, 37, 39
Liberation Tigers of Tamil Eelam, 36
Libya, 18
LTSP, 15, 93, 94, 95, 99, 100, 101
LTTE, 36, 37, 38
Macedonia, 32
Malcolm X, 22
Mamdani
  Mahmood, 39
Mandela
  Nelson, 25
masters, 6, 11, 17, 67, 108
Mehdi
  Nisan, 50, 51
Metcalf
  Barbara, 28
  Thomas, 28
middle class, 8
migrated, 14, 45, 49, 102
migration, 2, 14, 44, 45, 46, 47, 51, 52, 59, 62, 63, 68, 100, 102, 106
Milosevic
  Slobodan, 32, 33, 34
Moghul, 27
Mohammedanism, 27
money, 70, 98
monopolists, 97
Montana, 14, 59, 62, 63, 80, 84, 86
Montenegro, 32, 47
Montgomery, 70
Moses, 26, 27, 54

Mountbatten
  Louis, 50
Muhammad, iii, 24, 28
Muslims, 26, 27, 28, 31, 32, 41, 49, 50, 51, 100
Myanmar, 41
NAACP, 15
NAN, 15
nation formation, 2, 14, 23, 40, 41, 43, 44, 45, 47, 51, 52, 88, 90, 91, 100, 101, 102, 103, 106, 107, 108, 109
National Urban League, 15
NATO, 34
Nimeiry
  Gaafar, 39
North America, iii, 1, 13, 20, 88, 103
North Dakota, 14, 59, 62, 63, 84, 86
Northern Ireland, 41
Obama
  Barack, 56
Oduho
  Joseph, 40
oligopolists, 97
oppressed, 23, 25, 26, 27, 28, 29, 31, 38, 39, 40, 41, 42
oppressor, 23, 25, 26, 27, 28, 29, 38, 39, 40, 41, 42
Ottoman Empire, 31
Pakistan, 28, 46, 49, 50, 51, 100
parthenogenesis, 14, 21
Partition, 2, 28, 44, 49, 50, 51, 52, 100
Pharaoh, 26

phenotype, 17
political parties, 93
poor, 8, 10, 16, 17, 104, 107
population, 3, 4, 28, 29, 31, 46, 47, 48, 50, 52, 54, 58, 59, 61, 62, 73, 76, 77, 79, 84, 86, 94, 100, 101, 105
power, 4, 7, 14, 15, 23, 24, 25, 26, 27, 28, 31, 32, 34, 38, 40, 41, 43, 67, 71, 105
Prabhakaran
   Velupillai, 36, 38
Presidential election, 106
Prosser
   Gabriel, 24
Protestants, 41
psychology, 7, 9, 95
Public Administration, 67
quandary, 8, 9, 21, 47
race, 17, 42, 106
racial minorities, 40
racism, 8, 20, 103
racist, 16, 47, 54, 60
Rajapaksa
   Mahinda, 37
Reconstruction, iii, 11
reparationists, 3
reparations, 3, 18, 53, 89, 91, 94, 101, 102, 103
Republika Srpska, 33, 34
Revelations, 24
Rhode Island, 59, 62
Robinson
   Brooks, i, 1, 18, 53, 88, 89, 90, 97
   Lindsey "Rob", 1
Rohingyas, 41
Roman Catholics, 32

Rosewood, Florida, 23
Rwanda, 26, 29, 30, 31, 41
Rwandan Patriotic Front, 30
same-sex couples, 104
satan, 73
Say's Law, 64
Senate Bill 1038, 89
Sengupta
   Somini, 37
Serbia, 32, 33, 47
Serbians, 31, 33
Serbs, 31, 32, 33, 34, 35
sexual addiction, 10
Shabazzland/Zion, 21, 44, 51, 52, 88, 91, 93, 94, 95, 96, 97, 98, 100, 101, 103
Shastri
   Amita, 37
Sinhalese, 26, 35, 36, 39, 41
slave, 1, 2, 5, 6, 10, 13, 14, 19, 21, 25
slavery, 1, 5, 6, 44
Slovenia, 32
socioeconomic, 17, 88, 91, 94, 95, 99, 100
Socratic Method, 8
Sodom and Gomorrah, 24
South Dakota, 14, 59, 62, 63, 80, 84, 86
South Sudan, 40, 47
Spanish, 45
Spear
   Percival, 28
sports addiction, 10
Sri Lanka, 26, 35, 36, 37, 38, 41
Stavis
   Ben, 35
Sudan, 39, 40, 47

Sudan People Liberation
   Army, 40
Takeconomics, 53, 54, 73
Tamil New Tigers, 36
Tamils, 26, 35, 36, 41
territorial grab, 56, 58, 59,
   60, 61, 63, 72, 76
territories, 3, 45, 49, 51, 53,
   55, 57, 58, 60, 61, 62, 64,
   65, 66, 67, 68, 69, 70, 71,
   72, 73, 74, 100
Tito
   Josip Broz, 32
TNT, 36
Trailways, 69
Transportation, 69, 80, 81
Tudjman
   Franjo, 33
Tulsa, Oklahoma, 23
Ture
   Kwame, 24
Turner
   Nat, 24
Tutsis, 26, 29, 30, 31, 41
Uighurs, 41
UN, 34, 38, 45, 47
United Nations, 33, 34, 45,
   46, 48
United States, iv, 11, 19, 23,
   46, 48, 80, 89
US, 2, 12, 44, 46, 48, 51,
   52, 53, 54, 55, 56, 57, 58,
   59, 61, 67, 68, 70, 71, 74,
   75, 82, 89, 90, 91, 93, 94,
   95, 101, 102
Ustasha, 32
Vansina
   Jan, 29
vegetarianism, 65

Vermont, 59, 62
Vesey
   Denmark, 24
videogame addiction, 10
Vietnam, 18
Vojvodina, 32
wealth, 8, 29, 38, 52, 90, 97,
   98, 99
WEBEX, 89
West
   Cornel, 8
Western Civilization, 108
Western media, 72
Western World, 12, 107
White America, 1, 3, 5, 7,
   10, 13, 14, 16, 18, 19, 20,
   22, 43, 54, 62, 64, 67,
   108, 109
White Americans, 1, 22, 54,
   70, 90, 105, 109
White Supremacy, 20, 108
Whites, 2, 8, 18, 51, 54, 59,
   61, 76
Wholesale/Retail Services,
   72
Wilmington, North
   Carolina, 23
Wolpert
   Stanley, 28
Wyoming, 14, 59, 62, 63,
   80, 84, 86
XXX While Black, 8
Yahweh, 26
Yanga
   Joseph Lagu, 39, 40
Yoruba Culture, 20
Yugoslavia, 31, 32, 33
ZOOM, 89
Zurgas, 39

www.ingramcontent.com/pod-product-compliance
Lightning Source LLC
Chambersburg PA
CBHW070652220526
45466CB00001B/399